AF690838

101 Ways

To Protect Yourself Online

Simple Everyday Habits to Keep Your Identity, Money, and Privacy Safe

By

Dr. Ousmane Barry

PhD in Cybersecurity with AI and ML focus

Helping everyday people stay safe in a connected world.

PUBLISHED BY

Dr. Ousmane Barry

United States

2025

COPYRIGHT

Copyright © 2025 by Dr. Ousmane Barry

All rights reserved.

This book is licensed for personal use only. No part of this publication may be reproduced, stored in a retrieval system, or transmitted in any form or by any means, including electronic, mechanical, photocopying, recording, or otherwise, without prior written permission from the author, except for brief quotations used in reviews, education, or commentary.

DISCLAIMER

This book is for educational and informational purposes only. While every effort has been made to ensure accuracy, cybersecurity risks evolve, and situations may vary. This book does not serve legal, financial, or professional cybersecurity consulting. Readers should consult qualified professionals for personal or organizational security decisions. The author is not responsible for any actions taken based on the information in this book.

DEDICATION

For everyone who believes safety begins with awareness.

This book is for the everyday person who wants to feel in control of their digital life.

You do not need to be a cybersecurity expert to protect yourself online.

You only need the willingness to learn, the courage to question what feels unsafe, and the confidence to take small steps that make a big difference.

Table of Contents

INTRODUCTION

We live in a connected world. Every day, we use the internet without even thinking about it. We send messages, scroll through social media, buy things online, check our bank accounts, store our memories in the cloud, handle work emails, and keep in touch with the people we care about. Technology has become part of our daily routine, just like eating, sleeping, or breathing.

But with that connection comes exposure.

The same tools that make life easier can also create risks. A single careless click can expose your email. A weak password can give someone access to your bank account. A personal detail shared online can reveal more about your life than you realize. And sometimes, you may not even know anything happened until it's too late.

Many people believe cybercrime is something that happens to "other people." People who are careless. People who are not tech-savvy. People who don't pay attention.

But the truth is different.

Most people who get hacked or scammed are simply people who were never taught how to protect themselves. Nobody explained what to look for. Nobody showed them the signs. Nobody gave them the steps. Cybersecurity has been treated as something too complicated for everyday life, hidden behind technical language and specialized knowledge.

It doesn't have to be that way.

Staying safe online is not about being paranoid. It's not about living in fear, avoiding technology, or hiding from the modern world. It's about understanding how to protect yourself the same way you lock your doors, check your bank statements, or teach a child to look both ways before crossing the street.

Safety comes from habits.

This book is here to give you those habits: small, practical steps that are easy to use and easy to remember. You don't need to be technical. You don't need expensive tools. You don't need to change your life. You just need awareness, consistency, and confidence.

Why I Wrote This Book

I wrote this book because I have seen the consequences of not knowing these habits. I have seen people lose access to their email and, with it, every other account they owned. I have seen families struggle after someone stole their identity. I have seen teenagers get blackmailed after sharing something they thought was private. I have seen business owners lose money to digital scams that look completely legitimate.

And in many of those situations, the person blamed themselves.

"I should have known better."

"I feel stupid."

"I don't know how this even happened."

But it was never their fault.

They were simply never taught.

My goal is to teach you what most people were never shown. To give you clarity instead of confusion. To help you understand *how* and *why* things happen, and most importantly, how to prevent them.

What You Will Learn

By the end of this book, you will be able to:

1. Protect your identity and personal information online
2. Secure your accounts and prevent unauthorized access
3. Recognize financial scams and avoid losing money
4. Safeguard your privacy and reputation

5. Keep your family, your home, and your digital life secure

Each of the 101 steps in this book is concrete and actionable. You can start using them today, no matter what your experience level.

Who This Book Is For

This book is for people who use the internet.

Which means this book is for almost everyone.

It is for parents who want to protect their children.

It is for professionals who rely on their online presence.

It is for students just beginning to build their digital identity.

It is for older adults learning how to navigate online communication.

It is for business owners who want to protect their customers and reputation.

It is for individuals who have already experienced a digital problem and those who want to avoid one.

If you use a phone, a computer, social media, a bank app, or email, this book was written with you in mind.

Let's Get Started

You deserve to feel safe online. You deserve to make confident choices. You deserve peace of mind.

Technology is not something to fear. It is something to understand.

Once you understand it, you can control it.

This is your starting point.

One chapter at a time.

One habit at a time.

Let's begin.

CHAPTER 1
Protect Your Identity and Personal Life

1. Share Less Personal Information Online

What It Means:

Your online presence reflects your real life. When you post personal details about where you live, where you work, your birthday, your family, or your daily routines, you create a digital map of your life. Scammers and identity thieves collect these details to guess passwords, impersonate you, or access your accounts. Most people overshare online without realizing how much they are revealing.

How to Protect Yourself:

1. Think before you post. Ask yourself, *Does the public need to know this?*
2. Avoid sharing your full birthday, phone number, address, travel plans, or daily habits.
3. Set your social media accounts to Private where possible.
4. Only accept friend or follower requests from people you know in real life.
5. Review older posts and remove anything that gives away too much detail.

If It Happens:

1. Delete or hide posts that reveal sensitive personal information.
2. Change your privacy settings on social platforms to limit who can see future posts.
3. Search your name online and request removal of content that exposes personal details.
4. If someone is using your information, contact the platform and report impersonation immediately.
5. Consider activating identity monitoring services to watch for misuse of your name or data.

2. Avoid Posting Your Location in Real Time

What It Means:

Sharing where you are at the moment can seem harmless, but it can expose you to risks. When you post that you are at the gym, at a restaurant, traveling, or away from home, you may be signaling that your home is empty or that you are in a vulnerable situation. People with harmful intentions can use this information to target you online or in person.

How to Protect Yourself:

1. Post photos and updates after you leave a location, not while you are still there.
2. Turn off location tagging on your phone camera.
3. Do not allow social media apps to share your location automatically.
4. Be cautious when using check-ins or tagging places.
5. Teach children and teens this habit as well.

If It Happens:

1. Remove the post or update that reveals your current location.
2. Review the privacy settings of your apps to ensure location data is off by default.
3. If you believe someone is stalking, following, or monitoring you, document all posts, messages, and interactions. Then report this to the platform, your local authorities, or a trusted professional.
4. Let friends or family know if you feel unsafe, so you are not dealing with it alone.

You deserve to move freely without being watched. Delaying your posts by even one hour can significantly reduce your risk.

3. Keep Your Home Address Private

What It Means:

Your home address is one of the most sensitive pieces of personal information you have. When someone knows your address, they can link it to your name, your family, your workplace, and even your financial accounts. Many people accidentally expose their address without realizing it through posted mail photos, delivery photos, online resumes, or public records sites.

How to Protect Yourself:

1. Do not post photos of packages, mail, or front-door deliveries unless the address is completely covered.
2. Avoid entering your address into websites that seem unfamiliar or untrustworthy.
3. When possible, use a P.O. Box or package locker for online orders.
4. Remove your home address from public profiles and social media bios.
5. Be cautious when filling out online forms. If it is not required, leave it blank.

Examples:

1. If you want to post a photo of a new package, cover the label with your hand before taking the picture.
2. If a form asks for your address, but it is not required (like a newsletter signup), do not enter it.

If It Happens:

1. Delete any posts or online content that show your full address.
2. Search for your name and address online. Request removal from sites that publish personal data.

3. If mail is being opened or stolen, contact your local postal service to report mail tampering.
4. If you feel unsafe, consider changing package delivery to a P.O. Box or secure pickup location.
5. Inform trusted neighbors to watch for suspicious activity around your home.

Your home should be a place of safety. Keeping your address private protects your peace.

4. Use Separate Emails for Important and Everyday Accounts

What It Means:

Your email address is often the gateway to everything you do online. If someone gets access to your primary email, they can reset passwords, read personal messages, and take control of your most important accounts. Many people use the same email for everything, which increases the risk. By separating your email addresses by purpose, you reduce the damage someone can cause if one account is compromised.

How to Protect Yourself:

1. Use one email for your financial accounts, medical portals, banking, taxes, and government-related logins.
2. Use a different email for social media, streaming services, shopping accounts, and newsletters.
3. Avoid linking your work email to personal accounts.
4. Create a new, clean email if your current one has been used everywhere.
5. Turn on security alerts for both email accounts so you are notified if someone tries to access them.

Examples:

1. Important Email: Bank account, credit card account, tax website, health insurance login.
2. Everyday Email: Online shopping, loyalty programs, food delivery apps, social media sign-ins.

If It Happens:

1. If your email was accessed by someone else, immediately change the password to a strong, unique one.
2. Check if your recovery email and phone number were changed. If so, restore them.
3. Review your social media, banking, and other accounts for unusual login activity.
4. Enable two-factor authentication on your email accounts to prevent future unauthorized access.
5. If you can no longer access the account, use the provider's account recovery tool to regain control.

Using two email addresses is a small habit that creates a powerful layer of protection.

5. Be Careful With Social Media Games and Quizzes

What It Means:

Those fun quizzes that ask what character you are, what your personality type is, or what your birthday means may seem harmless. However, many of these games are created to collect personal information. The questions often match common security questions used to recover accounts, such as your childhood pet's name, your favorite teacher, your birthplace, or your mother's maiden name.

Once someone has those details, they can attempt to reset your passwords or impersonate you.

How to Protect Yourself:

1. Do not answer games or quizzes that ask for personal history details.
2. Be cautious with quizzes shared in group chats or trending on social media.
3. Avoid connecting these apps to your Facebook, Google, or email login.
4. Ignore links to quizzes from unknown websites or pages you do not recognize.
5. Teach friends and family that these quizzes often collect private information.

Examples:

1. "What was your first pet's name?" appears in quizzes and also in bank security questions.
2. "What city were you born in?" can be used to reset a password if someone tries to impersonate you.

If It Happens:

1. Delete quiz apps or permissions from your social media account settings.
2. Change your security questions wherever possible to answers only you would know.
3. Consider using answers that are not real but are memorable to you.
4. For example, if the question is "Mother's maiden name," choose something unrelated but consistent.
5. Monitor your email for alerts that someone is trying to reset your accounts.

The less personal history you share online, the harder it is for someone to pretend to be you.

6. Limit Personal Details in Public Profiles

What It Means:

Your public profiles are often the first places people look when learning about you. If your profile shows your workplace, school, hometown, birthday, or relationship status, it becomes easier for someone to guess your passwords, answer security questions, or impersonate you. Most people share more than they realize simply because profiles automatically ask for information.

You have the right to decide what is private. You do not owe the internet your personal life.

How to Protect Yourself:

1. Review your profiles on social media, shopping accounts, and forums.
2. Remove details like your full birthday, home city, workplace, or phone number.
3. Use general descriptions instead of specifics. For example, instead of "Works at ABC Hospital," try "Healthcare Professional."
4. Keep your friend or follower list private.
5. Avoid linking accounts together across platforms.

Examples:

1. Instead of listing your high school or graduation year, leave that section blank.
2. Instead of showing your exact job title, list your field (for example, "Education" or "Technology").

If It Happens:

1. Edit your profiles to remove identifying information.
2. Use privacy settings to hide details from the public.
3. Search your name online to see what others can see.

4. If your information is on data collection sites, request removal. Many sites have forms for this.
5. If someone is impersonating you, report the fake account immediately to the platform.

Key Idea:

The less personal information available publicly, the harder it is for someone to use it against you.

7. Use a Different Birthday on Public Accounts

What It Means:

Your real birthday is often used to verify your identity. It appears in banking, healthcare, employment records, and government documents. If your real birthday is visible online, someone could use it to reset accounts or answer identity questions. Many people list their real birthday on social media without realizing it increases their risk.

The goal is not to hide who you are. The goal is to avoid giving away information that can be used to prove you *are* you.

How to Protect Yourself:

1. Use your real birthday only on accounts that require legal identity, such as banking and taxes.
2. For social media or entertainment apps, choose a different day and month.
3. If a website requires your birthday to allow access (such as age restrictions), use a memorable but different date.
4. Avoid posting "birthday celebration" photos that show the exact date and year.

Examples:

1. If your real birthday is July 14, use July 10 or June 14 on social media accounts.
2. If you want to celebrate online, post: "Feeling grateful today" instead of the exact date.

If It Happens:

1. Edit your profiles to update the birthday to a different date.
2. Review old posts to remove "Happy Birthday on [Month Day]" comments that reveal the date.

3. If someone has already used your birthday to attempt identity fraud, contact your bank and credit bureaus to place a fraud alert.
4. Monitor your account notifications for unusual activity.

Key Idea:

Your real birthday belongs in private records, not public profiles. Changing it online helps protect your identity.

8. Treat Your Phone Number as Private

What It Means:

Your phone number is more powerful than most people realize. It is often connected to your email, bank login, social media accounts, and two-factor authentication codes. If someone gets your phone number, they may try to spam or scam you or even attempt to take over your accounts through SIM swapping, which transfers your number to their phone. Your phone number is not just a contact detail. It is a key to your digital identity.

How to Protect Yourself:

1. Only give your phone number to people and businesses you trust.
2. Do not post your phone number on social media profiles, websites, or message boards.
3. Avoid using your phone number to sign into new apps. Choose email sign-in instead.
4. Turn on a SIM card PIN so no one can move your number to another device without your permission.
5. Use two-factor authentication apps instead of SMS codes when possible.

Examples:

1. If a website wants your phone number for "discounts" or "offers," skip the offer and keep your number private.
2. If someone messages you asking for your phone number to "verify your identity," do not give it.

If It Happens:

1. Contact your mobile carrier immediately if you notice your phone signal suddenly stops working or your number is not connecting.
2. Change passwords for all accounts linked to your phone number.
3. Enable two-factor authentication using an app instead of text messages.
4. Inform your bank and credit card companies to watch for suspicious activity.
5. Consider updating your phone number if spam or fraud attempts become frequent.

Key Idea:

Your phone number is a valuable piece of your identity. Treat it like sensitive information, not a casual detail.

9. Remove Old Accounts You No Longer Use

What It Means:

Every account you create online holds pieces of your personal information. Even if you no longer use the account, the data remains stored somewhere. Old accounts are easier targets for hackers because they often have weak passwords, outdated security settings, or inactive users who do not notice when something is wrong. The fewer accounts you have, the less exposed you are.

How to Protect Yourself:

1. Make a list of old accounts you remember using, such as old email accounts, shopping sites, gaming accounts, or forums.
2. Log in and delete or deactivate accounts you no longer need.
3. If you cannot remember the login information, use password recovery tools or search your email for account confirmations.
4. Moving forward, only create accounts you actually plan to use.

Examples:

1. If you once created an account for a streaming trial and never used it again, delete it.
2. If you signed up for an app two years ago and forgot about it, remove it along with the app itself.

If It Happens:

1. If an old account has been accessed without your permission, reset the password immediately.
2. Remove any personal details stored in the account.
3. Change passwords for any active accounts that use the same or a similar password.

4. If financial information is linked, notify your bank to watch for suspicious charges.
5. Consider using a password manager to keep track of current accounts only.

Key Idea:

The fewer accounts you have online, the harder it is for someone to access your personal information or identity.

10. Review Photos Before Posting Them

What It Means:

Photos often reveal more than we notice. A picture taken at home can show your house number, street signs, family names, or personal documents in the background. A picture taken at work can show your badge, computer screen, or company details. Even reflections in mirrors or windows can expose private information. Looking closely before posting helps protect your privacy without changing what you share.

How to Protect Yourself:

1. Pause and look at the background of every photo before posting.
2. Check for house numbers, street names, license plates, or school logos.
3. Avoid taking photos in front of computer screens or personal mail.
4. Use your phone's built-in edit tools to crop or blur sensitive details.
5. Turn off location tagging in your camera settings.

Examples:

1. If you take a picture of a new key, cover the teeth of the key so no one can copy it.
2. If you want to show a new car, crop out the license plate before posting.
3. If you take selfies at work, make sure your ID badge is not visible.

If It Happens:

1. Delete any photos that reveal sensitive information.
2. If someone reposted your photo without permission, request removal from the platform.

3. If your home address or workplace is now public, change privacy settings on your accounts.
4. Tell family members and friends to use the same habit of reviewing photos before posting.

Key Idea:

A quick moment to review a photo can prevent personal information from being shared with strangers.

11. Be Cautious When Talking About Your Job Online

What It Means:

Your workplace is part of your identity, but sharing too much about it can put you at risk. When people know where you work, what you do, and who you report to, they can use that information to scam you, your coworkers, or even your employer. Many online scams start with small pieces of workplace information gathered from social media.

It is not about hiding your job. It is about protecting your professional and personal safety.

How to Protect Yourself:

1. Share your profession in general terms instead of naming your exact company or location.
2. Avoid posting photos of your workplace, computer screens, or ID badges.
3. Do not discuss workplace issues, internal policies, or private conversations online.
4. If you post about work achievements, keep the details simple and positive.
5. Never share schedules, travel plans, or upcoming projects publicly.

Examples:

1. Instead of saying "Nurse at City General Hospital," you can say "Healthcare professional."
2. Instead of posting a photo inside your office, take the picture in a neutral area away from screens or documents.

If It Happens:

1. Remove posts that reveal sensitive workplace information.
2. Notify your employer if you think someone is impersonating you or using your job information in a scam.
3. Block and report accounts that pressure you for insider details.
4. If you post a badge or document, request new credentials if possible.
5. Remind coworkers to avoid sharing workplace discussions publicly.

Key Idea:

Your job is part of your life, but it doesn't need to be fully visible online. Protecting your workplace information also protects your personal safety.

12. Do Not Share Your Travel Plans Publicly

What It Means:

Sharing that you are traveling can unintentionally signal that your home is empty. Posting vacation dates, flight information, hotel photos, or airport check-ins in real time can pose risks, including break-ins, identity theft, and stalking. Even if your account is private, posts can still spread or be seen by people you did not intend to see them.

You can still celebrate your travels. The key is to share it after you return.

How to Protect Yourself:

1. Avoid posting your departure dates, flight times, or hotel locations while you are away.
2. Wait to share vacation photos until you are back home.
3. Tell only trusted friends or family members about your travel schedule.
4. Turn off location tagging in your camera and social media apps.
5. Be cautious with travel countdown posts.

Examples:

1. Instead of posting "Off to Miami for the week," post photos when you are already home.
2. If your children are included in travel pictures, share them privately with close family instead of publicly.

If It Happens:

1. If you already posted travel plans, remove the posts or set them to private.
2. Ask a trusted neighbor or family member to check your home while you are away.

3. If you believe your home was targeted, do not enter alone. Contact local authorities first.
4. After returning home, review your privacy settings to prevent future exposure.

Key Idea:

Enjoy your experiences fully. Share the memories later. Your safety is worth the delay.

13. Avoid Sharing Children's Information Online

What It Means:

Children cannot protect their privacy on their own. When their names, birthdates, school locations, schedules, or photos are shared online, that information can stay online permanently. Strangers may learn personal details about your child, including where they live, where they learn, and when they are away from home. Even well-intentioned posts can create long-term digital footprints that children did not choose.

Protecting children online is about giving them safety now and freedom later.

How to Protect Yourself:

1. Do not post full names, birthdates, or school names in photos or captions.
2. Avoid sharing daily routines such as school pick-up times or after-school activities.
3. When sharing photos, make sure backgrounds do not reveal locations or identifying details.
4. Consider sharing pictures privately with family and close friends instead of posting publicly.
5. Teach children simple online safety habits as they grow, such as not sharing their address or school.

Examples:

1. Instead of posting a photo of a child in front of the school sign, take the photo indoors or in a neutral area.
2. If you want to share a birthday photo, do not include a cake with their full name on it.

If It Happens:

1. Remove or make private any posts that share identifying information.
2. Request that family and friends do the same if they shared similar content.
3. If your child's information appears on data collection sites, request removal.
4. If someone is contacting or messaging your child online, block the account and report it.
5. Talk openly with your child about what happened and reassure them that they are safe.

Key Idea:

Children deserve privacy. What we share about them today can affect their safety and freedom tomorrow.

14. Be Selective With Friend Requests

What It Means:

Not everyone who sends you a friend request or follow request is who they claim to be. Some accounts are created to steal information, send harmful links, or gather details about your life. Accepting unknown requests can expose your personal posts, your family, your location, and your daily routines.

Being careful about who you connect with protects your privacy and your peace of mind.

How to Protect Yourself:

1. Only accept friend or follower requests from people you know in real life.
2. If you receive a request from someone you know but the profile looks new or unusual, contact them directly to confirm.
3. Do not accept requests from accounts with no profile photo, very few posts, or usernames that look random.
4. Review your friend or follower list regularly and remove people you do not recognize.
5. Set your social media profiles to private when possible.

Examples:

1. If you see two profiles with the same name and picture, one may be a fake copy.
2. If someone says, "I found you online, let's connect," but you have never met, ignore the request.

If It Happens:

1. If you accepted a suspicious request, remove or block the account immediately.
2. Change your privacy settings so that future posts are visible only to trusted contacts.

3. If an unknown account messages you, do not click any links or share personal information.
4. If the account impersonates someone you know, report it to the platform for removal.
5. Inform your real contacts so they are aware and can avoid the fake account.

Key Idea:

Your online circle should be made up of people you trust. Protect your space by being selective.

15. Search Yourself Online Regularly

What It Means:

Your online presence is constantly changing, sometimes without your awareness. Information about you may appear on social media, public websites, data collection services, old accounts, or even posts made by other people. Searching your own name helps you see what others can see. It gives you the chance to remove or correct information before it creates problems.

This is about awareness, not fear. Knowing what is online about you gives you control.

How to Protect Yourself:

1. Type your name and phone number into a search engine and review the results.
2. Try searching for your name with your city, workplace, or social usernames to see what appears.
3. Check image results as well as text results.
4. If you see old accounts, unwanted photos, or outdated information, take steps to remove them.
5. Repeat this check every few months. It only takes a few minutes.

Examples:

1. If you search for your name and find an old profile you forgot about, log in and delete it.
2. If you see your name listed on a data collection site, request removal. Many offer a simple form.

If It Happens:

1. If you find inaccurate or harmful information, document it and request a correction or removal.
2. If someone is using your name without permission, report the account or page immediately.
3. If your personal information appears in a public directory, contact the site to request removal.
4. If private images or content appear online, contact the platform's removal team. Many sites handle this quickly.
5. If you feel overwhelmed, take it one step at a time. You do not need to fix everything in one day.

Key Idea:

Regularly searching your own name helps you stay aware of your digital presence and protect your privacy.

CHAPTER 2
Secure Your Accounts and Logins

16. Use Strong, Unique Passwords

What It Means:

Your password is the lock on your digital life. Just like you would not use the same key for your home, car, office, and mailbox, you should not use the same password for all your accounts. If one password is compromised, every account that uses that same password becomes vulnerable.

Hackers do not guess passwords manually. They use automated tools that test billions of password combinations every second. Short, simple, or reused passwords are quickly compromised. Long and unique passwords stop those attacks in their tracks.

How to Protect Yourself:

1. Use passwords that are at least 12–16 characters long.
2. Combine unrelated words, numbers, and symbols that mean nothing to others but are easy for you to remember.
3. Avoid personal information like birthdays, nicknames, favorite sports teams, or pet names.
4. Never reuse passwords across accounts. Every important account should have its own password.
5. Consider using a password manager to create and store secure passwords automatically.

Examples:

1. Weak password: Michael1995
2. Strong password: QuietCandleGreenWindow47$@
3. Strong password (random): N*4sTqP9h!2eRs84

If It Happens:

1. If you learn someone accessed your account, change the password immediately.
2. Change passwords for any accounts that use the same or similar passwords.
3. Turn on two-factor authentication to prevent future unauthorized access.
4. Review account activity to confirm nothing has been modified.

Key Idea:

A strong and unique password is one of the easiest and most effective ways to secure your online identity.

17. Turn On Two-Factor Authentication

What It Means:

Two-factor authentication (often called 2FA) means that logging in requires two steps: something you know (your password) and something you have (a code or authentication app). Even if someone steals your password, they usually cannot access your account without that second step.

This one habit significantly reduces the chance of someone breaking into your accounts.

How to Protect Yourself:

1. Turn on two-factor authentication for your most important accounts first (email, banking, social media).
2. Whenever possible, use an authentication app instead of text message codes because apps are more complex to intercept.
3. Keep your backup codes in a safe place in case you lose your device.
4. Enable login alerts so you receive notifications if someone tries to sign in.

Examples:

1. Authentication apps: Google Authenticator, Authy, Microsoft Authenticator.
2. Security keys (even stronger protection): YubiKey, Google Titan.

If It Happens:

1. If you receive a login code you did not request, someone may be trying to access your account. Change your password immediately.
2. If you lose access to your phone, use your backup codes to log in and reset your authentication settings.

3. If your account is accessed, review recent activity and disconnect unfamiliar devices.

Key Idea:

Two-factor authentication adds a powerful extra layer of protection, making your accounts far harder to break into.

18. Use a Password Manager

What It Means:

Most people cannot remember dozens of long, unique passwords. That's why password managers exist. They securely store your passwords and generate strong ones for you. You only need to remember one master password. The password manager does the rest.

This makes it much easier to stay secure without memorizing anything complicated.

How to Protect Yourself:

1. Choose a reputable password manager from a trusted company.
2. Create a master password that is long, memorable, and not tied to personal information.
3. Let the password manager generate new passwords for your accounts.
4. Use the manager on both your phone and your computer so you always have access.
5. Turn on two-factor authentication for the password manager itself.

Examples:

1. Recommended password managers: Bitwarden, 1Password, Dashlane, Keeper.
2. Master password idea: Instead of "MyDog," use "QuieTmoRninGreadingCoffee8@1."

If It Happens:

1. If you suspect your password manager is compromised, change your master password immediately.
2. Update any weak passwords stored in the manager.

3. Use your backup recovery key to restore access if you're locked out.

Key Idea:

A password manager strengthens your security while making your online life easier to manage.

19. Change Passwords After a Data Breach

What It Means:

When a company gets hacked, your login information may be leaked. Hackers often post or sell this data online. They then try your password across other websites to see where else it works. This is why using unique passwords matters.

If a company reports a data breach, act quickly.

How to Protect Yourself:

1. Sign up for breach notifications at: haveibeenpwned.com
2. If your account is listed in a breach, change the password immediately.
3. Also, change passwords for any accounts that use the same password.
4. Turn on two-factor authentication for all affected accounts.
5. Monitor financial accounts for unusual activity after a breach.

Examples:

1. If your shopping account is breached, update your email password as well if they were similar.
2. If your email is breached, assume all connected accounts may be affected.

If It Happens:

1. Change passwords right away.
2. Review login activity for each account.
3. Notify your bank if your financial accounts are connected.
4. Freeze your credit if identity theft is suspected.

Key Idea:

Acting quickly after a breach prevents a minor issue from becoming a serious problem.

20. Use Backup Codes for Important Accounts

What It Means:

Backup codes are one-time codes that let you log in to an account if you lose access to your phone or authentication device. They are your emergency key. Without backup codes, being locked out of your phone could mean being locked out of everything.

How to Protect Yourself:

1. Generate backup codes for important accounts such as email, banking, and password managers.
2. Store them in a safe place such as a secure folder, printed copy, or password manager.
3. Do not screenshot backup codes or store them in your phone's notes app.
4. Update backup codes when you change authentication settings.

Examples:

1. Print backup codes and keep them in a sealed envelope in a safe location.
2. Store backup codes in your password manager under a clearly labeled entry.

If It Happens:

1. Use a backup code to regain access to your account.
2. Once logged in, update your authentication method and generate new backup codes.
3. If you cannot regain access, contact the support team of the service for identity verification.

Key Idea:

Backup codes ensure you stay in control of your accounts even if something unexpected happens.

21. Review Account Permissions Regularly

What It Means:

Over time, your accounts may become connected to apps, websites, and devices you no longer use. These connections are often created when you sign in using "Continue with Google" or "Sign in with Facebook," or when you allow an app to access your camera, contacts, or location. If these apps are not secure or you stop using them, they can become weak points in your security.

Reviewing permissions helps you maintain control over who has access to your data.

How to Protect Yourself:

1. Check the list of apps connected to your social media and email accounts. Remove any you do not recognize or no longer use.
2. Review your phone's app permissions. Disable access to location, microphone, camera, and contacts when they are not needed.
3. Avoid using "Sign in with Facebook" or similar shortcuts unless necessary. Create separate logins instead.
4. Review browser extensions and remove any that are unnecessary.
5. Repeat this check every few months to ensure your accounts stay secure.

Examples:

1. If you downloaded a photo editing app but no longer use it, remove its access to your photos or delete it entirely.
2. If you install browser extensions to shop or find deals, remove them when you are done using them.

If It Happens:

1. If you find an app or service you do not recognize, remove its access immediately.
2. Change your account password in case the connected service was malicious.
3. Review recent activity in your account to make sure nothing has been modified.
4. Turn on two-factor authentication if it is not already enabled.

Key Idea:

Your accounts may be connected to more apps than you realize. Regular reviews keep your data in your hands.

22. Do Not Save Passwords in Your Browser

What It Means:

Most web browsers offer to save your passwords for convenience. However, if someone gains access to your computer, they can view or export all those passwords in seconds. Browser-saved passwords are also more vulnerable to malware that targets stored credentials.

Using a password manager is safer because it encrypts your passwords and requires a master password to access them.

How to Protect Yourself:

1. Turn off the setting that allows your browser to save passwords.
2. Use a dedicated password manager to store login details securely.
3. Log out of your accounts when you are done using shared or public computers.
4. Lock your device with a strong passcode or fingerprint so others cannot access your files.
5. Clear old passwords stored in your browser once you move to a password manager.

Examples:

1. Instead of letting Chrome save your banking password, store it in a password manager.
2. If you use public computers, always check that no passwords were saved by accident.

If It Happens:

1. If your browser has saved passwords, export or delete them and move them to your password manager.
2. Change passwords for any accounts accessed from shared devices.

3. Review your browser's security settings and disable automatic password storage.
4. Run a malware scan to ensure your device is clean.

Key Idea:

Storing passwords in a password manager keeps them protected. Storing them in your browser leaves them exposed.

23. Log Out of Devices You No Longer Use

What It Means:

Many people keep multiple devices logged into apps and websites. Over time, these may include old phones, tablets, shared laptops, gaming consoles, or borrowed computers. Staying logged in gives anyone with access to those devices the ability to see your messages, photos, or private accounts.

Logging out removes the open door.

How to Protect Yourself:

1. Review your account's active sessions. Most major platforms let you see all devices currently logged in.
2. Log out of devices you do not use often.
3. After upgrading your phone or computer, log out of the old one before selling, giving away, or recycling it.
4. Use screen locks on all devices to prevent unauthorized access.
5. Reset your passwords if you are unsure whether an old device is still logged in.

Examples:

1. Email services like Gmail let you view all active sessions and sign out remotely.
2. Streaming accounts often show all connected devices.

If It Happens:

1. Log out of all devices from your account settings.
2. Change your password to prevent re-entry.
3. If the device was lost or stolen, use device locator tools to erase your data remotely.
4. Notify your service provider if personal or financial accounts are involved.

Key Idea:

Every device you stay logged into is a doorway. Make sure only the ones you trust remain open.

24. Avoid Using the Same Username Everywhere

What It Means:

Many people use the same username across different websites and apps. While it may feel convenient, it also makes it easier to track you online. If someone learns your username on one platform, they can search for it on others. This can reveal your accounts, hobbies, location clues, and who you interact with. In some cases, a username can even be linked back to your real identity.

Using different usernames helps separate your online accounts and makes it harder for strangers or attackers to connect with your digital activity.

How to Protect Yourself:

1. Use one username for casual or public accounts and a different one for private or personal accounts.
2. When signing up for important accounts such as banking, insurance, or medical services, avoid using usernames that are used anywhere else.
3. Do not include personal information in your username, such as your name, birthday, school, or city.
4. Consider using a password manager to store usernames along with passwords to keep everything organized.
5. If an account allows you to change your username, update it to something more private.

Examples:

1. Instead of using "JohnDoe85" everywhere, use different usernames like "calmreadingforest" for one site and "clearbluewindow" for another.
2. If your favorite game username is used publicly, do not reuse it on your email or bank account.

If It Happens:

1. If you realize your username is too personal or used in too many places, choose a new one and update accounts gradually.
2. Search your username online to see where it appears. Remove or update accounts you no longer use.
3. If someone has connected your accounts through your username, check each account's privacy settings and adjust them.
4. If you receive unwanted messages or harassment, block the user and report the account on that platform.

Key Idea:

Your username is part of your online identity. Keeping it unique and separate helps protect your privacy.

25. Opt Out of Data Brokers and People-Search Websites

What It Means:

Your personal information is often collected and sold by data brokers. These sites may show your full name, phone number, home address, relatives, and past locations. This makes it easier for scammers, stalkers, and identity thieves to find you. Removing your information reduces your exposure and protects your privacy.

How to Protect Yourself:

1. Search for your name on people-search sites like Whitepages, Spokeo, and TruePeopleSearch.
2. Use each site's "Remove" or "Opt-Out" request form.
3. Repeat this for major data brokers or use services that automate removal.
4. Repeat every few months because data often reappears.
5. Consider using a PO Box or work address for deliveries and registrations going forward.

If It Happens:

1. Remove your data immediately from the site.
2. Freeze your credit if any signs of identity misuse appear.
3. Change your phone number if you become targeted and the harassment escalates.
4. Keep a record of where you've removed your data for easier updates later.

Key Idea:

The less of your identity that is publicly searchable, the harder it is for someone to target you.

26. Use a Secure Email Provider

What It Means:

Not all email services offer the same level of security. Some providers collect data about you, scan your messages, or offer weak protection against hackers. A secure email provider protects your privacy, uses strong encryption, and guards against unauthorized access.

Email is the foundation of your digital identity. Choosing a secure provider gives you stronger protection from the start.

How to Protect Yourself:

1. Choose an email service that focuses on privacy and security rather than advertising.
2. Look for providers that offer encryption, two-factor authentication, and strong security controls by default.
3. Avoid using your work or school email for personal accounts, as they can be monitored or suspended.
4. Store backup codes for your secure email in a safe location.
5. Regularly review your account recovery options to make sure they are accurate and secure.

Examples of Secure Email Providers:

1. Proton Mail
2. Tutanota
3. Zoho Mail (privacy-focused business email)

These services are designed to protect user data rather than profit from it.

If It Happens:

1. If you suspect someone accessed your email, change your password immediately.
2. Turn on two-factor authentication if it is not already enabled.
3. Review recent login history and remove any unfamiliar devices.
4. Update recovery phone numbers and emails to ensure they belong only to you.
5. If your account was used to send messages you did not write, notify your contacts to avoid misleading links.

Key Idea:

Your email provider should protect your privacy, not compromise it. Choosing a secure email service strengthens your entire online foundation.

27. Enable Login Alerts on All Accounts

What It Means:

Login alerts notify you when someone signs into your account from a new device, location, or browser. If you receive an alert and you are not the one who logged in, it is an early warning sign that someone may be trying to access your account. Early awareness allows you to act before damage occurs.

This simple setting can stop a problem before it becomes serious.

How to Protect Yourself:

1. Turn on login alerts for email, banking, social media, cloud storage, and any accounts you consider essential.
2. Set alerts to notify you through both email and text if possible.
3. Review alerts immediately. Do not ignore them.
4. If you do not recognize a login, act quickly by changing your password and enabling two-factor authentication.
5. Check your account's security page to remove any unknown device sessions.

Examples:

1. If you receive an alert saying, "New login from another location," and you were not traveling, this is a sign of unauthorized access.
2. If you see login attempts listed in your security activity, even unsuccessful ones, change your password.

If It Happens:

1. Change your password for that account right away.
2. Turn on two-factor authentication if it is not already enabled.

3. Sign out of all sessions and remove any devices you do not recognize.
4. Review your account recovery information and update it if needed.
5. If the account is financial, notify your bank or provider to watch for suspicious activity.

Key Idea:

Login alerts act as your early warning system. They help you respond quickly before your personal information is misused.

28. Avoid Public or Shared Email Recovery Accounts

What It Means:

Your recovery email is used to reset your passwords and confirm your identity. If your recovery email is weak, shared, old, or rarely checked, your entire online identity becomes easier to compromise. Someone could reset your passwords without you knowing.

Think of your recovery email as the master key. It must be private and secure.

How to Protect Yourself:

1. Do not use a shared family email as your recovery email.
2. Do not use an old email address you no longer monitor.
3. Use a secure, private email address that only you control.
4. Turn on two-factor authentication for your recovery email.
5. Check your recovery email account regularly to ensure it is active and safe.

Examples:

1. If you created an email years ago and no longer log into it, do not use it as a recovery email.
2. If your partner or sibling also knows the password to your recovery account, create a new private one.

If It Happens:

1. If you find that your recovery email is insecure, update your account settings immediately and add a secure email.
2. Change the password for your recovery email and enable two-factor authentication.

3. Review which accounts use the old recovery email and update them one by one.
4. Remove outdated recovery emails that no longer belong to you.
5. Check for password reset attempts you did not request.

Key Idea:

Your recovery email should be your most secure email. It protects everything connected to it.

29. Do Not Use Your Phone Number As Your Primary Account Recovery Method

What It Means:

Many accounts let you regain access by sending a code to your phone number. While this seems convenient, phone numbers can be taken over through scams, SIM swapping, or carrier errors. If someone takes control of your phone number, they could reset your passwords and access your accounts without knowing them.

Relying only on a phone number creates a single point of failure. It is safer to use a secure email and authentication app.

How to Protect Yourself:

1. Use a secure email as your primary recovery method instead of your phone number.
2. Turn on two-factor authentication that uses an authentication app instead of text messages.
3. Contact your phone carrier and request extra security on your account, such as a separate PIN for changes.
4. Be cautious when sharing your phone number online or on forms.
5. Avoid linking your phone number to services that do not require it.

Examples:

1. If a service asks: "Use phone number for password recovery?" choose "Use email instead."
2. Use Authenticator apps rather than text message codes whenever possible.

If It Happens:

1. If your phone number is taken over, contact your carrier immediately and request a SIM lock and account freeze.
2. Change passwords for accounts that use your phone number for recovery.
3. Switch your account recovery settings to a secure email and authentication app.
4. Review login activity for any unusual access attempts.
5. Notify your bank if financial accounts are connected to your phone.

Key Idea:

Your phone number is too easy to steal to be your primary recovery method. Use a secure email and authentication app for stronger protection.

30. Use Physical Security Keys for Your Most Sensitive Accounts

What It Means:

A security key is a small physical device that you plug into your computer or tap on your phone to confirm your identity when logging in. It is one of the strongest forms of protection available. Even if someone knows your password, they cannot access your account without the physical key. This protects you from phishing, hacking, and most account takeover attempts.

Security keys are handy for email, banking, social media, work accounts, and any other accounts that involve your identity or finances.

How to Protect Yourself:

1. Use a security key for your primary email account and any account that is critical to your daily life.
2. Buy keys from trusted companies that specialize in security.
3. Set up at least two security keys: one for everyday use and one as a backup stored safely.
4. Store your backup key in a safe place at home, not on a keychain or in a bag you carry around.
5. Register your keys in your account settings under security or login protection.

Examples:

1. Common brands: YubiKey and Google Titan.
2. Plug the key into your computer or tap it on your phone to confirm your login.

If It Happens:

1. If you lose your primary security key, use your backup key to log in and register a new key.
2. If both keys are lost, use your backup codes to regain access.
3. Once back in your account, remove the lost keys from your security settings.
4. Review recent account activity to ensure no unauthorized actions occurred.
5. Replace the lost key quickly to stay protected.

Key Idea:

A security key provides one of the strongest levels of protection for your most valuable accounts.

31. Use a Separate Device for Sensitive Accounts

What It Means:

The more apps, downloads, and activities you use on a single device, the greater the chance of something going wrong. If you use the same phone or computer for banking, shopping, gaming, social media, and browsing random websites, a single infection or compromise could affect all of them.

Using a separate device for your most important accounts reduces the risk. This could be an older phone, a tablet, or a simple laptop that you use only for banking, work, taxes, or medical accounts.

It does not need to be expensive. It only needs to be clean and used carefully.

How to Protect Yourself:

1. Choose one device to use only for essential tasks such as banking, email, and official accounts.
2. Do not install social media, gaming apps, or unnecessary software on this device.
3. Do not browse suspicious websites or download files on this device.
4. Keep the device updated with the latest security patches.
5. Use a strong password and lock the device when not in use.

Examples:

1. Use your primary phone for everyday social media and communication.
2. Use a separate, simple tablet or spare phone only for login to banking and financial accounts.

If It Happens:

1. If your primary everyday device gets hacked, your financial and personal accounts remain safe on a separate device.
2. If the secure device is lost or stolen, change the passwords for any accounts used on it.
3. Use device tracking tools to erase the device remotely if possible.
4. Replace the secure device and restore access carefully, focusing on keeping it clean.

Key Idea:

Separating your everyday device from your secure device adds a strong layer of protection without needing technical skills.

32. Avoid Logging Into Important Accounts on Shared or Public Computers

What It Means:

Shared or public computers are often found in libraries, schools, hotels, workplaces, and computer labs. Many people can use these devices, and you cannot be certain how they are maintained. They may have outdated security, hidden malware, or keystroke-logging software. Logging in to your banking, email, or other personal accounts on these computers can expose your passwords and private information.

When a computer is not yours, assume it is not secure.

How to Protect Yourself:

1. Only sign into sensitive accounts on devices that you trust and control.
2. If you must use a shared computer, avoid typing passwords or accessing financial or personal accounts.
3. Use your phone instead whenever possible, even if it is less convenient.
4. Never choose the option to "remember my password" or save login info on a shared computer.
5. Always log out completely when you are finished.

Examples:

1. Do not check your bank account from a hotel business center computer.
2. Use your smartphone hotspot instead of using a public computer to manage essential accounts.

If It Happens:

1. If you log into an essential account on a shared computer, change your password as soon as possible.
2. Enable two-factor authentication on the account if it is not already enabled.
3. Review your account activity to make sure nothing has been changed.
4. If you suspect the computer was compromised, log out of all devices from your account settings.
5. Run security checks on your personal devices to ensure they remain safe.

Key Idea:

If the device is not yours, do not trust it with your most important information.

33. Clear Saved Logins and Browsing Data on Devices You Share

What It Means:

When you share a computer, tablet, or phone with others, your accounts and personal information can easily be left behind. Websites may keep you logged in. Browsers may store your passwords. Search history may remain visible. Anyone who uses the device after you can access your accounts without needing your password.

Clearing login information and browsing data protects your privacy whenever a device is shared.

How to Protect Yourself:

1. Always log out of your accounts when using a shared device.
2. Open private or incognito mode when you browse, so data is not stored.
3. Do not save passwords when the browser asks.
4. After using the shared device, clear browsing history, cookies, and saved logins.
5. If possible, use your own device instead of shared ones for personal accounts.

Examples:

1. When using a family computer, log out of your email before closing the browser.
2. At work, avoid signing in to personal accounts on your office computer unless necessary.

If It Happens:

1. If you think someone may have accessed your account, change the password immediately.
2. Enable two-factor authentication for additional protection.
3. Review recent account activity to confirm nothing has changed.
4. Remove old devices from your account's logged-in list.
5. Talk with family or others who use the device about respecting each other's privacy.

Key Idea:

Shared devices require extra care. Always remove your digital footprints when you are done.

34. Set Up Recovery Questions You Do Not Share Publicly

What It Means:

Many accounts ask security questions such as your mother's maiden name, your first pet's name, your hometown, or your favorite teacher. These questions are meant to confirm your identity. However, the answers are often easy to guess or find online. If someone knows you or can view your social media, they may already know these answers.

Treat security questions like extra passwords. The answers should not be real or easy to discover.

How to Protect Yourself:

1. Do not use real answers for recovery questions. Use made-up answers that only you know.
2. Store your recovery answers in your password manager so you do not forget them.
3. Choose answers that do not appear anywhere online or in conversation.
4. Avoid security questions that use information others could easily know or find.
5. If your account allows you to choose your own security question, choose one that is personal and private.

Examples:

1. Real: Mother's maiden name is Johnson.
2. Secure: Answer could be "blueglassriverpath" (completely unrelated).
3. Real: First pet's name is Bella.
4. Secure: Answer could be "skywatermintroad."

Your answers do not need to make sense. They only need to be consistent.

If It Happens:

1. If someone reset your account using security questions, change the password immediately.
2. Update all security questions with new, private answers.
3. Turn on two-factor authentication if it is not already enabled.
4. Review account recovery emails and phone numbers to ensure they belong only to you.
5. Check login activity to confirm the account is now secure.

Key Idea:

Recovery questions are passwords in disguise; use answers no one else could ever guess.

35. Adopt Passkeys and Phishing-Resistant Login Methods

What It Means:

Passwords can be stolen, guessed, reused, or tricked out of you through phishing scams. Passkeys are a newer login method that replaces passwords with secure digital keys stored on your device. You sign in using Face ID, fingerprint, or your device PIN. There is no password to type, no password to steal, and no password for attackers to trick you into entering.

How to Protect Yourself:

1. Turn on passkeys for websites and apps that support them (Google, Apple, Microsoft, PayPal, etc.).
2. Use your fingerprint, Face ID, or device PIN to unlock your passkey.
3. Let your password manager sync and store your passkeys securely across devices.
4. When logging in, select "Use Passkey" instead of typing a password.
5. Reduce reliance on SMS/phone-based codes, which can be intercepted.

Examples:

1. Choose "Sign in with Passkey" when signing into your Google account instead of entering a password.
2. Enable biometric login (Face ID, Touch ID) for banking apps when prompted.
3. Use a password manager that supports passkeys for backup and device syncing.

If It Happens:

1. If you lose your phone or laptop, remove the lost device from your account's trusted device list immediately.
2. Keep at least one backup sign-in method (another device, hardware security key, or printed recovery code).
3. If you must temporarily use a password, ensure it is long and unique, so it is not a weak link.

Key Idea:

Passwords can be stolen. Passkeys can't. Switching to passkeys adds one of the strongest layers of security available today.

CHAPTER 3
Secure Your Devices and Software

36. Avoid Using Social Media Accounts to Sign Into Other Websites

What It Means:

Many websites let you create an account with "Sign in with Facebook," "Sign in with Google," or similar options. While this seems faster, it creates a chain connection between your accounts. If someone gains access to your social media or email account, they can instantly access every account linked to it. Also, these sign-ins allow companies to share data about your activity, habits, and interests.

Keeping your accounts separate prevents one breach from spreading to others.

How to Protect Yourself:

1. When creating new accounts, use your email and a unique password instead of linking to social media login.
2. Review websites where you already used social sign-in and convert them to email-and-password login when possible.
3. Check the list of connected apps inside your social media and email accounts and remove any you do not use.
4. Use a password manager to remember login details instead of relying on account linking.

Examples:

1. Instead of "Continue with Facebook," choose "Create account with email."
2. If your social media is ever hacked, linked accounts could be at risk. Separate them ahead of time.

If It Happens:

1. If your social media or email account is compromised, change the password immediately.
2. Go to your social account's "connected apps" or "linked websites" section and remove any unfamiliar or unnecessary connections.
3. Convert linked accounts to direct email logins by using the "reset password" feature on those websites.
4. Turn on two-factor authentication to strengthen protection going forward.

Key Idea:

Your accounts should not be connected like a chain. Keep them separate to protect your digital identity.

37. Avoid Public Wi-Fi or Use a VPN

What It Means:

Public Wi-Fi networks in places like airports, hotels, restaurants, or shopping centers are convenient, but they are not secure. Anyone connected to the same network could try to intercept your browsing activity, login details, or personal information. A VPN (Virtual Private Network) creates a private, encrypted connection so others on the same network cannot see what you are doing.

How to Protect Yourself:

5. Avoid entering passwords or accessing important accounts when on public Wi-Fi
6. Do not access your banking, email, or work accounts on an unsecured network
7. Use your phone's mobile data hotspot instead of public Wi-Fi when possible
8. If you must use public Wi-Fi, turn on a VPN before browsing
9. Choose a trusted VPN provider with a good privacy reputation

Examples:

1. If you are in a café and want to check your bank account, switch to your phone's hotspot instead of using the café Wi-Fi
2. When traveling, connect to hotel Wi-Fi only to download needed information, then disconnect

If It Happens:

1. If you logged in to essential accounts on unsecured Wi-Fi, change your passwords right away
2. Check your email and financial accounts for any unusual login activity

3. Turn on two-factor authentication for all important accounts
4. Run a malware scan on your device if anything feels suspicious
5. Use a VPN moving forward whenever you are not on a private network you trust

Key Idea:

Public Wi-Fi is never fully safe. If you must use it, protect yourself with a VPN or use your mobile hotspot instead.

38. Do Not Store Credit Card Information on Shopping Websites

What It Means:

Many online stores offer to save your credit card information for faster checkout. While this is convenient, it also increases your risk. If the website is hacked, your stored card information could be exposed. Even well-known stores are targeted by cybercriminals because they hold valuable financial data.

By choosing not to store payment information, you reduce the amount that can be stolen.

How to Protect Yourself:

1. Enter your card details manually each time you make a purchase.
2. Use a secure digital wallet (such as Apple Pay or Google Pay) where your card number is not actually shared with the merchant.
3. If a website insists on saving your card, consider shopping elsewhere.
4. Check your bank statements regularly for purchases you do not recognize.
5. Use a credit card rather than a debit card for online purchases because credit cards offer stronger fraud protection.

Examples:

1. Instead of clicking "Save card for faster checkout," select "Do not save."
2. If you shop frequently, use a digital wallet that protects your real card number.

If It Happens:

1. If you suspect your card information was exposed, contact your bank immediately.
2. Request a new card number or a replacement card.
3. Review recent transactions and report any you did not make.
4. Change the password for your shopping account and remove stored payment details.
5. If identity theft is suspected, consider freezing your credit to prevent new accounts from being opened in your name.

Key Idea:

Convenience should never outweigh safety. Entering your card information manually keeps your financial details protected.

39. Use Virtual or Single-Use Card Numbers for Online Purchases

What It Means:

Some banks and credit card companies allow you to create a temporary card number that can be used for online purchases. This number differs from your actual card number. If the website where you shop gets hacked, only the temporary number is exposed, not your primary card. This provides strong protection against fraud.

Using virtual card numbers is like wearing gloves: it adds a protective layer between your finances and the internet.

How to Protect Yourself:

1. Check if your bank or credit card provider offers virtual or disposable card numbers.
2. Use a virtual card number when shopping online, especially on new or unfamiliar websites.
3. Set spending limits on each virtual card to reduce financial exposure.
4. Use a new virtual card number each time when possible.
5. Monitor your statements regularly, just as you would with your regular card.

Examples:

1. Some banks show a button in your online account for "Generate Virtual Card."
2. Services like Capital One, Citi, Bank of America, Apple Card, and privacy.com offer virtual card options.
3. You can create a temporary number for a one-time purchase, then delete it afterward.

If It Happens:

1. If a virtual card number is stolen, deactivate that virtual card. Your real card remains safe.
2. If fraudulent purchases occur, report them to your bank and request a new virtual card number.
3. Review associated accounts where the virtual card was used and remove it from those websites.
4. If the breach affected your email or shopping account, change your passwords and add two-factor authentication.

Key Idea:

Virtual cards act as a shield. They prevent your real financial information from ever being exposed online.

40. Use Credit Instead of Debit for Online Transactions

What It Means:

When you shop online, using a credit card is safer than using a debit card. Strong fraud policies protect a credit card. If someone uses your card without your permission, you can dispute the charges and avoid paying for them. A debit card directly withdraws money from your bank account. If your debit card is stolen or misused, your money may be gone before you notice the problem. Recovering funds from a lost debit card can take longer and be more difficult.

Using a credit card helps you protect your money before it is spent.

How to Protect Yourself:

1. Use a credit card, not a debit card, when shopping online.
2. Use virtual or single-use card numbers when available.
3. Turn on transaction alerts so you are notified when your credit card is used.
4. Review your monthly statement to confirm every purchase is valid.
5. If a credit card number is compromised, request a replacement card immediately.

Examples:

1. If you need to purchase on a new website, use your credit card for the transaction.
2. If your debit card is linked to subscriptions or automatic payments, switch them to your credit card for added protection.

If It Happens:

1. If your credit card number is misused, call the card company right away. They can reverse unauthorized charges.
2. Request a new card number to replace the compromised one.
3. Review your bank account and credit report for any additional suspicious activity.
4. If your debit card is used fraudulently, contact your bank. The refund process may take time, so act quickly.

Key Idea:

Using a credit card for online purchases protects your money. A debit card puts your bank account directly at risk.

41. Use a Separate Bank Account for Online Purchases

What It Means:

If you use the same bank account for daily expenses, savings, bills, and online purchases, one security incident could affect everything. If your card or banking information is stolen, your main funds could be at risk. Separating your online spending from your main account limits the amount of money that can be accessed if something goes wrong.

This gives you control. Even if one account is compromised, the rest of your money remains safe.

How to Protect Yourself:

1. Open a second banking account to use only for online purchases.
2. Transfer money into this account only when needed.
3. Keep a low balance in this online spending account.
4. Do not link this account to automatic bill payments or savings.
5. Use this account's debit or virtual card for online shopping.

Examples:

1. If you usually keep $3,000 in your primary account, keep only $100–$300 in your online spending account.
2. When you shop online, transfer the exact amount needed into the separate account before making the purchase.

If It Happens:

1. If your online spending card is stolen, lock the card and report it to your bank.
2. Replace the card and continue using the separate account system.

3. Review transactions and dispute any you did not make.
4. Because this account has limited funds, your main savings and checking accounts remain protected.
5. Change your online account passwords if financial fraud occurs.

Key Idea:

Separating your online spending from your main money adds a strong layer of financial protection.

42. Create Strong PINs and Passcodes for All Devices

What It Means:

Your phone, tablet, and computer are gateways to your personal information. If someone gains access to your device, they can read your messages, open your email, reset your passwords, or access your financial accounts. A weak PIN or passcode makes this much easier. Using a strong passcode helps keep your devices and identity secure.

A strong passcode does not need to be complex. It just needs to be hard for others to guess.

How to Protect Yourself:

1. Use at least a 6-digit PIN on your phone. Avoid simple combinations like 123456 or 111111.
2. Consider using a longer passcode instead of a PIN, such as a short phrase you can remember.
3. Avoid birthdays, anniversaries, or numbers connected to your personal life.
4. Turn on fingerprint or face recognition for convenience and added protection.
5. Make sure every device you own is locked when not in use.

Examples:

1. Instead of using your birthday, choose something that has no connection to you personally.
2. A strong passcode could be something like 284965 or a phrase such as bookgreenmorning.

If It Happens:

1. If you think someone knows your passcode, change it immediately.
2. Review device security settings and enable biometric locks (fingerprint or face recognition).
3. If your device is lost or stolen, use the device tracking feature to lock or erase it remotely.
4. Change passwords for accounts that were logged in on the device.
5. Notify your bank if financial apps were accessible.

Key Idea:

A strong passcode protects your device, your identity, and your personal information.

43. Do Not Share Device Unlock Codes with Anyone

What It Means:

Your device unlock code is the key to everything stored on your phone, tablet, or computer. If someone knows your passcode, they could read your messages, open your email, view your photos, and access your accounts. Even people you trust may not handle your information with the same level of care you do. Once someone knows your passcode, it is no longer secure.

Keeping your device's unlock code private protects your privacy and identity.

How to Protect Yourself:

1. Do not share your device passcode with friends, coworkers, or relatives.
2. If someone needs to use your phone, unlock it yourself and hand it to them.
3. If a child regularly uses your device, create a separate guest or child account with limited permissions.
4. Change your passcode immediately if someone else learns it.
5. Use biometric locks, such as fingerprint or face recognition, for added security.

Examples:

1. If someone asks to borrow your phone to make a call, unlock the phone and dial the number for them.
2. If family members share a tablet, set up individual user profiles instead of sharing one unlock code.

If It Happens:

1. If you think someone knows your passcode, change it to a new and unrelated one.
2. Check your apps for unusual activity or settings changes.
3. Review your accounts for new logins or password reset attempts.
4. Turn on two-factor authentication for your important accounts to prevent unauthorized access.
5. If a device was accessed without your permission, consider resetting it to factory settings and restoring only trusted apps and data.

Key Idea:

Your device unlock code should stay private. Once shared, it no longer protects you.

44. Do Not Leave Your Devices Unattended in Public Places

What It Means:

Phones, tablets, and laptops store personal messages, photos, and financial information and give you access to your accounts. Leaving a device alone, even for a few seconds, allows someone to take it, look through it, or install something harmful. Theft can happen quickly and quietly. Even if the device is returned, your data may have already been copied.

Treat your device like your wallet. Keep it with you at all times.

How to Protect Yourself:

1. Do not leave your phone on café tables, counters, gym lockers, work desks, or car seats.
2. Keep laptops in your sight when working in public spaces.
3. Use a shoulder bag, zipped pocket, or secure backpack to hold your device.
4. When at school or work, lock your device screen when stepping away, even for a moment.
5. Use device tracking features such as Find My iPhone or Find My Device.

Examples:

1. In a coffee shop, take your laptop with you if you go to pick up your order or use the restroom.
2. In a classroom or office, lock your device before standing up.

If It Happens:

1. If your device is missing, use the tracking app immediately.
2. If you cannot recover it quickly, remotely lock and erase the device.

3. Change passwords for your important accounts.
4. Review account activity for unusual logins or messages.
5. Notify your bank if financial apps were installed on the device.
6. File a police report if needed, especially for insurance claims.

Key Idea:

Your device holds your digital life. Keep it with you, locked, and never unattended.

45. Turn On Automatic Screen Lock

What It Means:

Automatic screen lock means your device will lock itself after a short period of inactivity. This prevents someone from picking up your device and accessing your information if you set it down or forget it somewhere. Without an automatic lock, your device is open to anyone who touches it.

This is one of the simplest and strongest protections you can enable.

How to Protect Yourself:

1. Go into your device settings and set your screen to lock after 30 seconds to 1 minute of inactivity.
2. Use a secure PIN, password, fingerprint, or face recognition to unlock it.
3. Make sure your device locks every time the screen turns off.
4. Test the lock to ensure it is working correctly.
5. Avoid using smart unlock features that keep your device unlocked based on location or connected Bluetooth devices.

Examples:

1. If your phone automatically locks when you put it down, someone cannot pick it up and look through your information.
2. If your laptop locks when you close the lid, your documents and emails stay protected.

If It Happens:

1. If you realize your device was left unlocked and someone might have accessed it, change your passcode immediately.
2. Review your apps, messages, and accounts for suspicious activity.
3. Change passwords for email and financial accounts if anything seems unusual.
4. Turn on two-factor authentication to prevent unauthorized logins.
5. If your device may have been tampered with, consider backing up essential data and doing a whole device reset.

Key Idea:

An automatic screen lock protects your device even when you are not thinking about it.

46. Keep Your Operating System and Apps Updated

What It Means:

Your phone, tablet, and computer need regular updates to stay secure. Updates fix security weaknesses that hackers try to exploit. If you skip updates, your device becomes more vulnerable to viruses, malware, and unauthorized access. Keeping your software updated is like repairing cracks in your house before someone tries to break in.

Updates protect your device, your data, and your identity.

How to Protect Yourself:

1. Turn on automatic updates for your phone, computer, and apps.
2. Restart your devices when prompted so updates can finish installing.
3. Remove apps you no longer use, so you have fewer apps to maintain.
4. Only download apps from trusted app stores and official websites.
5. Make updating your devices part of your routine, just like checking messages or email.

Examples:

1. When your phone shows "Software Update Available," install it instead of delaying.
2. If your computer asks to restart updates, save your work and restart.

If It Happens:

1. If your device becomes infected due to missing updates, update the system immediately.
2. Run a trusted antivirus or security scan to remove threats.
3. Change passwords for accounts accessed on the device.
4. Turn on automatic updates going forward so this does not happen again.
5. Consider backing up your data and resetting your device if it shows unusual behavior after infection.

Key Idea:

Updates close security gaps. Keeping your device updated is one of the simplest ways to stay protected.

47. Install Only Trusted and Official Apps

What It Means:

Apps can access a lot of information on your device. They may see your contacts, location, photos, messages, and sometimes even your keystrokes. When you download apps from unverified or unofficial sources, you risk installing malware or spyware. Even apps that look normal may be designed to steal your data or track your activity.

Only install apps from trusted stores to protect your device and personal information.

How to Protect Yourself:

1. Download apps only from official app stores such as Google Play or the Apple App Store.
2. Avoid downloading apps from links, pop-ups, or random websites.
3. Check user reviews and ratings before installing an app.
4. Look at the permissions an app requests and remove or deny any that are unnecessary.
5. Delete apps you no longer use.

Examples:

1. If an app wants access to your microphone, camera, location, or contacts but does not need them to function, deny the permission.
2. If a friend sends a link to a game outside the app store, do not install it.

If It Happens:

1. If you accidentally installed a suspicious app, delete it immediately.
2. Restart your device to stop any activity connected to the app.

3. Run a trusted security or antivirus scan.
4. Change the passwords for accounts you accessed while the app was installed.
5. Monitor your device and account activity for anything unusual.

Key Idea:

Only install apps from trusted sources. If an app is not verified, it is not worth the risk.

48. Review and Limit App Permissions Regularly

What It Means:

Apps often request access to features such as your camera, microphone, contacts, photos, location, or messages. Some of these permissions are necessary for the app to work, but many are not. When an app has more access than it needs, it can collect more information about you than you realize. Reviewing app permissions helps ensure apps only have access to what is required and nothing more.

This keeps your personal data private and reduces unnecessary tracking.

How to Protect Yourself:

1. Go to your phone or tablet's settings and open the section for App Permissions or Privacy Controls.
2. Review which apps have access to your camera, microphone, location, contacts, and storage.
3. Turn off any permissions that are not needed for the app to function.
4. If you are unsure whether an app needs a permission, deny it and see if the app still works normally.
5. Delete apps that request excessive or suspicious access.

Examples:

1. A flashlight app should not need your location.
2. A calculator app should not need access to your contacts.
3. A game should not need to record audio unless it clearly explains why.

If something feels unnecessary, it probably is.

If It Happens:

1. If you notice an app has been accessing more information than expected, revoke the permissions immediately.
2. Delete the app if you no longer trust it.
3. Clear your browser and device history to remove leftover tracking data.
4. Change passwords for any accounts accessed while the app had permissions.
5. Monitor your device and accounts for unusual activity.

Key Idea:

Apps should only have access to what they need. You control your data. Always review what apps are allowed to see and do

49. Avoid Posting Your Daily Schedule or Habits

What It Means:

Sharing routines, such as the times you leave for work, when you go to the gym, or when your home is usually empty, can unintentionally give strangers insight into your daily patterns. This information can be used for stalking, burglary, or unwanted monitoring. Even casual posts like "Heading out now" or "At my usual morning coffee spot" reveal predictable behavior that could be exploited.

This is especially important if you have a public social media profile or many followers you do not know personally.

How to Protect Yourself:

1. Avoid real-time posting. Share highlights after you've left a location, not while you're still there.
2. Do not publicly announce your morning or evening routines.
3. Turn off location tagging so your posts do not automatically reveal where you are.
4. Be cautious with check-in features or apps that display where you are at the moment.
5. If you want to share life updates, delay them or remove exact time/place details.

Examples:

1. Instead of posting "At the gym every morning at 6," you share your fitness progress without mentioning the time or location.
2. You wait until you are home to post about tonight's restaurant rather than posting while sitting at the table.
3. You avoid tagging your favorite café every day, so your daily routine is not recognizable.

If It Happens:

1. Remove or archive posts that reveal patterns over time.
2. Adjust your privacy settings so only close friends can view shared content.
3. Turn off location tracking on social apps and cameras.
4. Be cautious moving forward and vary your routines if needed.

Key Idea:

Your routine is part of your personal safety. When you stop broadcasting your daily patterns, you reduce the risk of being tracked or targeted by people with potentially malicious intentions.

50. Disable Autofill for Personal and Payment Information

What It Means:

Autofill is a feature in browsers and apps that stores your name, home address, phone number, and even credit card details so that forms can fill in automatically. While it's convenient, it also means your personal and financial information is stored in places you may not realize. If someone gains access to your device, even for a short moment, they could autofill your information on any website. Malware can also target stored autofill data.

Disabling autofill helps protect your identity and financial security.

How to Protect Yourself:

1. Open your browser settings and look for the Autofill or Payment Information section.
2. Turn off the option for saving addresses, phone numbers, and payment cards.
3. Delete any autofill entries already stored in your browser.
4. Store payment information in a secure mobile wallet or enter it manually when needed.
5. If you use a password manager, store personal information there instead, where it is encrypted.

Examples:

1. You shop online and manually enter your address each time instead of letting your browser fill it in.
2. You remove your stored credit card details from your browser and keep them in a secure digital wallet instead.
3. You stop your phone from auto-populating name and address fields on apps you do not fully trust.

If It Happens:

1. Remove any stored personal or payment details from your browser autofill settings.
2. If someone may have used a card, notify your bank and request a replacement.
3. Check your account statements for unusual charges.
4. Update your device passcode to something more substantial.
5. Turn on alerts for transactions so you are notified of spending in real time.

Key Idea:

Convenience should never come at the cost of security. When you disable autofill, you protect your identity and financial information from unauthorized use.

CHAPTER 4
Protect Your Money and Financial Safety

51. Never Send Money to Strangers or Unverified Sellers

What It Means:

Scammers create fake profiles, listings, invoices, and urgent stories to pressure you into sending money. Once the money is sent, it is often impossible to get it back. Unverified sellers can disappear after payment or send counterfeit or broken items. Protecting your money starts with slowing down and verifying who you are paying.

How to Protect Yourself:

1. Do not send money to people you have just met online, even if the story feels convincing
2. Only pay sellers on reputable platforms that offer buyer protection
3. Use traceable payment methods with dispute rights, such as credit cards or protected marketplaces
4. Avoid wire transfers, gift cards, crypto, and peer-to-peer "friends and family" payments for purchases
5. Verify the seller's identity, reviews, and history before paying
6. Be skeptical of deals that are far below market price or that demand immediate payment
7. Save all messages, invoices, item descriptions, and payment receipts

Examples:

1. A seller asks you to pay by gift card or wire transfer to "hold" the item. Decline and walk away
2. A social media account claims to be a brand rep and offers a significant discount if you pay off-platform. Refuse and buy only through the official site

3. A renter asks for a deposit before a viewing. Do not pay until you have verified the property and the landlord

If It Happens:

1. Contact your bank or card issuer immediately and dispute the transaction
2. If you used a marketplace with buyer protection, open a claim with all evidence attached
3. Report the scammer's profile, listing, email, or phone number to the platform
4. Save screenshots of chats, listings, and payment confirmations
5. If personal or financial details were shared, change passwords and monitor statements
6. Consider a credit freeze if identity information was exposed

Key Idea:

Genuine sellers can be verified and do not pressure you to pay through risky methods. If you cannot confirm who you are paying, do not send money.

52. Avoid "Investment" Offers on Social Media

What It Means:

Scammers often use social media to promote fake investment opportunities. They promise fast profits, guaranteed returns, or risk-free earnings. They may pose as experts, influencers, business owners, or even celebrities. Once you send money, the scammer disappears or pressures you to send more. Real investments do not guarantee quick or high returns.

How to Protect Yourself:

1. Do not trust investment offers that come through DMs, comments, or group chats
2. Be cautious of anyone asking you to send money, crypto, or gift cards
3. Do not believe screenshots of "proof" like deposit receipts or earnings charts
4. Verify investment companies through official websites and government registries
5. If it sounds too good to be true, it is
6. Speak to a licensed financial professional before investing your money

Examples:

1. Someone messages you, saying, "I turned $200 into $5,000 in one day. I can help you do it too." Block and delete
2. A profile claims they trade crypto for clients and only need you to "send your investment first." Walk away
3. A group post promises high returns from a "new guaranteed forex algorithm." Ignore the offer

If It Happens:

1. Stop communicating with the scammer immediately
2. Collect screenshots and proof of the conversation and payments
3. Contact your bank or card issuer and report the transaction
4. Report on the scammer's profile on the platform
5. If personal details are shared, change passwords and monitor your accounts
6. If you feel pressured or threatened, contact local authorities

Key Idea:

Real investments come from verified financial institutions and never promise fast or guaranteed profits.

53. Do Not Store Card Numbers in Shopping Apps

What It Means:

Shopping apps, food delivery apps, ride-sharing apps, ticket apps, and online marketplaces often ask if you want to "Save your card for faster checkout." It feels convenient, but it increases your financial risk. If your phone is stolen, an account is compromised, or the company that stores your card is hacked, your payment information could be misused.

Many security breaches occur when card data is stored across multiple systems. The fewer places your card number is saved, the safer your money is.

How to Protect Yourself:

1. Choose "Do Not Save Card" whenever you check out in apps.
2. If your card is already saved, open the app's Payment Settings or Wallet and remove it.
3. Use more secure payment alternatives that do not expose your real card number:

- Apple Pay
- Google Pay
- PayPal
- Virtual card numbers from your bank

4. Log out of shopping accounts when you finish using them.
5. Turn on transaction alerts for your bank and credit cards so you get notified instantly of any purchase

Examples:

1. When ordering groceries or takeout, manually enter your card instead of saving it.
2. If you shop online often, use Apple Pay or Google Pay because they use encrypted, one-time payment tokens.
3. If old apps still have your card stored, remove the card and delete the app if you no longer use it.

If It Happens:

If you notice a suspicious purchase:

1. Contact your bank immediately and dispute the charge.
2. Request a new card number if you believe your information was exposed.
3. Remove your card from every app where it was stored.
4. Change your password for the affected app and turn on two-factor authentication.
5. Monitor your accounts daily for at least 30 days.
6. If many accounts had card data saved, take time to review all the places your financial information is stored and reduce it where possible.

Key Idea:

The more apps that store your card number, the more places your financial information can leak. Enter your card only when needed and avoid saving it permanently. This one habit reduces a lot of avoidable risk.

54. Look for Secure Checkout (HTTPS)

What It Means:

When you enter payment information online, you want to be sure the connection is protected. Secure websites use **HTTPS** in their addresses. The **"S"** means your information is being encrypted. If a site only uses **HTTP**, your card number or personal details could be intercepted. This is one of the easiest and most effective security checks to make before buying anything online.

How to Protect Yourself:

1. Look at the website address in the browser's address bar before entering any personal or financial information.
2. Make sure the web address begins with **https://**.
3. Check for the **small lock icon** next to the web address.
4. If you do not see the lock icon or the "S," do **not** enter payment information.
5. Shop only with well-known and trusted retailers.
6. If you clicked a link from an email or social media, verify the website address carefully.
7. Take a moment to read the URL. Scammers often use slightly misspelled or look-alike addresses.

Examples:

1. **https://www.amazon.com** is secure.
2. **http://www.amazon-payment-center.co** is not secure and is likely a scam.
3. A site selling expensive products at unusually low prices without HTTPS is a strong warning sign.

If It Happens:

1. Contact your bank immediately.
2. Ask your bank to monitor your account or issue a new card.
3. Change any password you created on that site.
4. Review your credit card statements daily for suspicious charges.
5. Turn on transaction alerts so you receive instant notifications.

Key Idea:

If the website is not secure, do not trust it with your information. Always look for **HTTPS** and the lock icon before making a purchase.

55. Beware of Limited-Time "Pressure" Offers

What It Means:

Scammers try to create a sense of urgency, so you feel rushed into making a decision. They want you to act before you think. This is why they use phrases like:

1. "Offer expires in 10 minutes."
2. "Only two spots left"
3. "You must pay right now."
4. "Send payment before someone else takes it."
5. "Do not tell anyone else about this deal."

Real businesses want informed customers, Scammers want quick reactions. When someone applies pressure, it is almost always a sign of a scam.

How to Protect Yourself:

1. Slow down and take your time before making any purchase or payment.
2. Do not let someone rush you into sending money or personal information.
3. Search the product, company, or offer on your own instead of using their link.
4. Remember that if the offer is genuine, it will still be there after you think about it.
5. If someone gets upset because you want to verify details, that is a major red flag.
6. Talk to a friend or family member before sending money.

Examples:

1. A seller says, "Someone else is waiting. Pay now or lose the item." Genuine sellers do not force instant payment.
2. A website uses a countdown timer to push you to buy quickly. Many of these timers reset when you reload the page.
3. A message says you won a prize, but must pay a "release fee." Legitimate prizes never require payment.

If It Happens:

1. If you send money because you felt pressured, contact your bank or card issuer immediately.
2. Request a dispute or chargeback.
3. Save screenshots, messages, and receipts in case they are needed later.
4. Report the scammer's profile, website, or listing to the platform.
5. If you share personal details, change your account passwords and security questions.
6. Monitor your bank accounts for any unusual transactions.

Key Idea:

If someone tries to rush you, stop. Pressure is one of the strongest signs of a scam. Slowing down protects you.

56. Confirm Payment Requests Before Sending Money

What It Means:

Scammers often pretend to be someone you trust. They may send messages that appear to be from a coworker, friend, manager, family member, or your bank. They often claim there is an emergency or a need for quick payment. Before sending money, always confirm the request directly with the real person or organization using a separate communication method. If the message feels rushed, secretive, or emotional, pause and verify.

How to Protect Yourself:

1. If someone asks you to send money, call them directly to confirm first.
2. Do not reply to the message where the request came from.
3. Contact the person or business using an official number or verified website.
4. Be cautious if the request says "Do not tell anyone" or insists on secrecy.
5. Never send money because of fear, urgency, or guilt.
6. Make it a habit to verify every unexpected payment request.

Examples:

1. A "boss" texts: "Buy gift cards for a work event and send the codes." Call your boss. This is a common scam.
2. A "family member" message from a new number asking for emergency money. Call their usual number to check.
3. An email claims your bank needs your login to fix an issue. Call the bank using the number on the back of your card.

If It Happens:

1. If you send money, contact your bank right away and report possible fraud.
2. If gift cards are used, contact the card issuer immediately with the codes and receipts.
3. Report the scam on the platform where it occurred.
4. Save screenshots and timestamps as evidence.
5. Change passwords if you shared account access.
6. Let friends and family know so they can watch for impersonation attempts.

Key Idea:

Always verify payment requests using a different communication method. If the request is real, the person will understand you double-checking.

57. Understand Common Online Scams

What It Means:

Scammers use the same methods because they work. When you recognize common scam patterns, you can stop them before they cause harm. Most scams try to do one of three things:

1. Get your money
2. Steal your personal information
3. Gain access to your accounts

Once you learn the patterns, you'll start to recognize scams much more quickly.

Common Scams to Recognize:

1. Phishing Emails and Texts: Fake messages claiming to be from your bank, delivery service, employer, or government.
2. Tech Support Scams: Someone claims your device is infected and asks for remote access.
3. Prize or Lottery Scams: You are told you "won" something but must pay a fee to receive it.
4. Romance Scams: Someone pretends to build a relationship to gain trust and eventually money.
5. Fake Online Shops: Websites offering expensive items at unusually low prices with no intention of delivering.
6. Investment Scams: Promises of guaranteed profits or extremely high returns.
7. Family Emergency Scams: Someone pretends to be a relative in trouble and asks for urgent help.

How to Protect Yourself:

1. Be cautious of messages that create urgency, fear, guilt, or excitement.
2. Check email addresses carefully; many scams use slight misspellings.
3. Never click links in messages you were not expecting.
4. Do not download attachments from unknown senders.
5. If someone online asks for money, stop and verify before doing anything.
6. Research websites and read reviews before making purchases.
7. Talk to someone you trust before sending money or sharing personal details.

Examples:

1. A text says your package is on hold and gives a link. Instead, go directly to the delivery company's official website to look it up.
2. A new online friend suddenly claims they need money for a medical situation. This is a common warning sign of a romance scam.
3. A job offer that requires you to pay upfront for supplies or training is likely fake.

If It Happens:

1. Stop responding immediately.
2. Save screenshots, messages, and website links as evidence.
3. Change any passwords that may have been shared.
4. Report the scammer on the platform where it occurred.
5. Contact your bank to dispute or stop payments if money is sent.

6. Consider placing a credit freeze if personal identity details are exposed.

Key Idea:

Scammers rely on confusion and emotion. Once you recognize the signs, you remove their advantage.

58. Contact Banks Using Official Phone Numbers

What It Means:

Scammers often pretend to be your bank. They may call, text, or email you, claiming there is a problem with your account. Their goal is to get you to share personal information or send money. Even if the caller ID looks real, it can be faked. To stay safe, always contact your bank using the phone number printed on your debit card, credit card, or the bank's official website. Never trust phone numbers included in messages, emails, or links.

How to Protect Yourself:

1. If someone contacts you claiming to be from your bank, do not share any personal information.
2. Hang up and call the number on the back of your bank card instead.
3. Do not click links in bank-related emails or text messages.
4. Log in through your bank's official app or website to check for real alerts.
5. Set up account notifications so you receive updates directly from your bank.
6. Remember that your bank will never ask for your PIN, full password, or verification codes over the phone.

Examples:

1. A text says: "Your account has been locked. Call this number." Ignore it and call the bank using the number on your card.
2. A caller claims to be from the fraud department and asks for your password. Hang up immediately.

3. An email urges you to click a button to "secure your account." Delete it, then check your account in the official app.

If It Happens:

1. If you gave personal information, change your online banking password right away.
2. If you shared your card number, request a new card from your bank.
3. If you gave a verification code, contact your bank's fraud department immediately.
4. Watch your account for unfamiliar withdrawals or charges.
5. Turn on transaction alerts to receive notifications for every purchase.

Key Idea:

Always contact your bank using the official phone number. If the request is real, your bank will confirm it. If it's a scam, you'll avoid the loss.

59. Freeze Your Credit When Not Applying for Loans

What It Means:

Your credit report contains your full name, address history, Social Security number, and financial identity. If someone gains access to this information, they can open loans or credit cards in your name. A credit freeze prevents new accounts from being opened using your identity. It is one of the strongest defenses against identity theft. Freezing your credit is free, safe, and does not impact your credit score.

How to Protect Yourself:

1. If you are not currently applying for credit or financing, keep your credit frozen.
2. Freeze your credit separately with each main credit bureau: Equifax, Experian, and TransUnion.
3. When you freeze your credit, you will receive a PIN or password. Store it securely.
4. If you need to apply for a loan, unfreeze your credit briefly and then re-freeze it when it is finished.

How to Freeze Your Credit:

Visit these official websites directly by typing them yourself:

1. Equifax: equifax.com/personal/credit-report-services/
2. Experian: experian.com/freeze/center.html
3. TransUnion: transunion.com/credit-freeze

Examples:

1. If you are not planning major purchases this year, keep your credit freezing to block fraudulent accounts.
2. If a company you used experienced a data breach, freeze your credit as a safety step.

3. If you notice a credit check you do not recognize, freeze your credit and investigate immediately.

If It Happens:

1. If someone opened an account in your name, contact the lender and close the account.
2. File an identity theft report at IdentityTheft.gov or your country's equivalent resource.
3. Freeze your credit right away if it has not frozen already.
4. Change passwords for your financial accounts.
5. Check your credit reports regularly for new activity.

Key Idea:

A credit freeze prevents identity thieves from opening accounts in your name. It is one of the simplest and most effective steps you can take to protect yourself.

60. Set Up Account Alerts for All Transactions

What It Means:

Account alerts notify you right away when money is spent, moved, or withdrawn. They help you spot unauthorized charges immediately. If someone tries to use your card or log in, you'll be alerted. Banks and card companies can send alerts by text, email, or app notification. This is one of the fastest ways to detect fraud.

How to Protect Yourself:

1. Turn on transaction alerts in your bank or credit card app.
2. Enable alerts for every purchase.
3. Enable alerts for online transactions.
4. Enable alerts for ATM withdrawals.
5. Enable alerts for large purchases.
6. Enable alerts for failed login attempts.
7. Choose instant notifications instead of daily summaries.
8. Check your alerts and don't ignore them.
9. Set alerts on bank accounts, credit cards, and payment apps (PayPal, Cash App, Venmo, Apple Pay, Google Pay).

Examples:

1. You see a $1.00 charge you don't recognize. Small charges are often tests before bigger fraud.
2. You receive a failed login alert. Someone may be trying to access your account.
3. You see a purchase from another city or country. Your card may have been copied.

If It Happens:

1. Contact your bank or card company immediately.
2. Lock or replace your card.
3. Change your online banking password.

4. Turn on two-factor authentication.
5. Review recent transactions and dispute unfamiliar charges.
6. If a payment app is involved, contact the app's support and secure your device.

Key Idea:

Instant alerts help you catch fraud early. The sooner you spot suspicious activity, the sooner you can stop it.

CHAPTER 5
Protect Your Privacy and Location Data

61. Turn Off Location Services for Most Apps

What It Means:

Many apps request access to your location even when they do not need it. When an app tracks your location, it may be learned where you live, where you work, and your daily habits. That information can be shared with advertisers, sold to data brokers, or exposed in a data breach. Limiting location access protects your privacy and reduces unnecessary tracking.

How to Protect Yourself:

1. Open your device's privacy or location settings.
2. Review which apps have location permissions.
3. Change most apps to "While Using the App" or "Never."
4. Only allow constant location access for apps that clearly require it (maps, ride services).
5. Turn off "Location History" or "Location Timeline."
6. Avoid posting your real-time location on social media.

Examples:

1. A weather app does not need all-day tracking. Type your city manually.
2. A shopping app should not have access to your location at any time.
3. A photo may reveal your exact location if location metadata is still attached.

If It Happens:

1. Revoke location permissions from apps you do not trust.
2. Delete any app that tracks more than necessary.
3. Clear your device's stored location history.
4. Change passwords if the app is linked to your accounts.
5. Watch unusual behavior in apps or accounts.

Key Idea:

Your location is personal. Only share it when there is a clear and necessary reason.

62. Limit Who Can See Your "Last Seen" Online

What It Means:

Many messaging apps show when you were last active or are currently online. This might seem small, but it can reveal your routine, availability, and daily habits. It can also create pressure to respond quickly. Limiting who can see your activity protects your privacy and your peace of mind.

How to Protect Yourself:

1. Open your messaging app's privacy settings.
2. Change your "Last Seen" or "Activity Status" to No one, Contacts only, or Close friends only.
3. Turn off read receipts if you don't want others to know when you've viewed messages.
4. Apply the same settings in apps like Facebook, Instagram, and WhatsApp.
5. Remember, you do not need to be available all the time.

Examples:

1. A coworker should not be able to see when you're online outside work hours.
2. If someone pressures you to reply quickly, hiding your activity reduces that pressure.
3. If you are distancing from someone, removing your online status prevents them from monitoring you.

If It Happens:

1. If someone is tracking your online activity, change your privacy settings immediately.
2. Block or mute anyone who ignores your boundaries.
3. Turn off notifications when you need a break.
4. Report ongoing harassment to the platform.

Key Idea:

You decide when you are available. Limiting your online presence strengthens your privacy and protects your peace of mind.

63. Review Microphone and Camera Permissions

What It Means:

Many apps request access to your microphone or camera even when they do not need it. If an app has unnecessary access, it could record audio, take pictures, or gather background data without your awareness. Some apps may misuse this data or become dangerous if they are hacked. Regularly reviewing permissions protects your privacy and personal space.

How to Protect Yourself:

1. Open your device's privacy settings.
2. Go to the Microphone and Camera permission sections.
3. Review which apps have access.
4. Turn off access for apps that do not truly need it.
5. For messaging or video apps, choose Allow Only While Using rather than Always.
6. Be cautious when new apps request camera or microphone access right away.

Examples:

1. A flashlight app should not need a microphone or camera access.
2. A shopping app does not need permission to record audio.
3. Some social media apps request these permissions for advertising data, not just photos or calls.

If It Happens:

1. If you notice suspicious activity (camera light flickering, microphone indicator on), uninstall the app immediately.
2. Restart your device to stop active access.

3. Run a malware or security scan if your device supports one.
4. Change passwords for accounts linked to the device.
5. Keep your operating system updated to fix security vulnerabilities.

Key Idea:

Only allow camera and microphone access when it is truly necessary. Your privacy deserves protection.

64. Cover or Disable Smart Home Cameras When Needed

What It Means:

Smart home cameras, doorbells, baby monitors, and indoor security cameras can be useful, but they can also be hacked or accessed by unauthorized users. A camera pointed at your living space can reveal your routine, who lives with you, and when your home is empty. Covering or disabling cameras when you are home adds privacy and control.

How to Protect Yourself:

1. Change the default username and password on every smart camera.
2. Turn on two-factor authentication in the camera app.
3. Keep the camera's software and firmware updated.
4. Place indoor cameras only where they are truly needed, like entry points.
5. Cover or unplug cameras when you are relaxing, getting dressed, or sleeping.
6. Avoid installing cameras in bedrooms or bathrooms.
7. Choose baby monitors that use strong encryption and require passwords.

Examples:

1. Unplug or cover a living room camera when guests are over.
2. If a child has a camera in their room, disable it when not needed.
3. Use a strong Wi-Fi password and do not share camera access with others.

If It Happens:

1. If the camera moves or settings change unexpectedly, change your password immediately.
2. Log out of all devices and reset the camera to factory settings.
3. Update your Wi-Fi password and reconnect only trusted devices.
4. Remove unknown users or devices from the camera access list.
5. If private footage may have been viewed, contact the manufacturer's support team.

Key Idea:

Smart cameras are tools, not constant observers. Use them when they help you and disable them when privacy matters.

65. Avoid Using Your Real Name on Public Platforms

What It Means:

Using your real name online makes it easier for others to find personal information about you. It can reveal where you live and where you work and connect your social media accounts. This can expose your personal life to strangers, advertisers, scammers, or people with harmful intentions. Using a screen name helps protect your identity while still allowing you to participate online. This is not about hiding. It's about protecting your privacy.

How to Protect Yourself:

1. Use a nickname, initials, or a username instead of your full name.
2. Avoid using your birth year, hometown, or workplace in your username.
3. Keep your personal identity and professional identity separate.
4. If a platform requires your real name, keep it private from public view.
5. Do not link personal social accounts to public forums, gaming, or online communities.

Examples:

1. Instead of "MichaelJohnson2021," choose something like "MJay" or "QuietDayStudio."
2. Use a screen name when joining public discussion groups instead of your real Facebook profile.
3. When posting reviews or comments online, use a username that does not identify you.

If It Happens:

1. Change your display name in your account settings.
2. Remove your full name from bios and profile pages.
3. Delete old posts that contain personal details.
4. Switch social profiles to private and control who can follow or message you.
5. Search your full name online and request removal of anything that feels unsafe.

Key Idea:

Your name is personal. Use a username online to protect your privacy and keep your real identity secure.

66. Use Privacy-Focused Web Browsers

What It Means:

Most web browsers collect your browsing habits to build advertising profiles. This means companies track what you search, what you click, what you buy, and how long you stay on each website. A privacy-focused browser reduces this tracking, blocks hidden trackers, and keeps your browsing history more private. This gives you greater control over your online footprint.

How to Protect Yourself:

1. Consider using privacy-focused browsers like Brave, Firefox, or DuckDuckGo.
2. Turn on tracking protection in your browser settings.
3. Disable third-party cookies.
4. Use private browsing mode for sensitive searches.
5. Avoid signing into your browser with your email unless necessary.
6. Keep your browser updated to protect against security flaws.

Examples:

1. If you look at shoes on one website and see ads for them everywhere, your browser is tracking you.
2. If ads seem to match your private conversations or searches, your activity data is being collected.
3. Privacy browsers help block these trackers and reduce how much data companies gather about you.

If It Happens:

1. Clear your browser history, cookies, and cached data.
2. Log out of websites you stay signed into and change your passwords.

3. Remove extensions you do not recognize or no longer use.
4. If your browser seems compromised, uninstall it and reinstall it from the official site.
5. Avoid downloading extensions from unknown or untrusted sources.

Key Idea:

Your browser is your gateway to the internet. Choosing one that protects your privacy helps protect everything you do online.

67. Clear Your Browsing Data Regularly

What It Means:

Your browser saves the websites you visit, what you search for, downloads, and cookies that track you across different sites. While some of this helps pages load faster, it also allows companies, advertisers, and sometimes hackers to learn about your habits. Clearing your browsing data reduces tracking and removes saved login information that could be misused.

How to Protect Yourself:

1. Open your browser's Settings or Privacy menu.
2. Select Clear Browsing Data or Clear History.
3. Clear browsing history, cookies, and cached files.
4. Do this weekly, or daily for stronger privacy.
5. Use Private or Incognito mode for sensitive searches.
6. Avoid staying logged in to websites when you're not actively using them.

Examples:

1. If you share a computer, clearing data prevents others from seeing your searches.
2. Clearing cookies reduces targeted ads that follow you across the internet.
3. Always clear browsing data on public or shared computers (stores, libraries, hotels, airports).

If It Happens:

1. If you think someone checked your browsing history, clear it immediately.
2. Change passwords for any accounts you were logged into.
3. Turn on two-factor authentication for extra protection.

4. Run a malware scan if webpages start redirecting or behaving oddly.
5. Reset your browser to default if you notice unfamiliar extensions or toolbars.

Key Idea:

Your browsing history is personal. Clearing it regularly keeps your activity private and harder for others to track.

68. Use Private Search Engines

What It Means:

Most search engines track what you search, where you are, what you click, and how long you stay on pages. This data is used to build advertising profiles about you. Private search engines do not store your search history or personal information, which reduces tracking and gives you more control over your data.

How to Protect Yourself:

1. Use privacy-focused search engines like DuckDuckGo, Startpage, or Brave Search.
2. Set one of them as your default search engine in your browser settings.
3. Avoid being logged into Google or other accounts while searching if privacy is important to you.
4. Use Private or Incognito mode for sensitive searches.
5. You can still use Google for complex searches but use private search engines for everyday browsing.

Examples:

1. Searching for medical symptoms on a regular engine may cause related ads to appear.
2. A private search engine does not save or share what you searched.
3. When researching products, private search prevents ads from following you across websites.

If It Happens:

1. If ads seem to know too much about you, switch to a private search engine.
2. Clear your browsing history and cookies to remove past tracking.

3. Check which accounts you are signed into while browsing.
4. Remove browser extensions you do not recognize.

Key Idea:

Your searches reveal personal details about your life. Using a private search engine helps keep that information from being collected or used for profit.

69. Control Who Can See Your Contacts and Photos

What It Means:

Many apps ask for access to your contacts or photo library even when they do not need it. Allowing this access can expose your personal relationships, your location history, and private moments. Some apps upload your contact list to their servers or scan photos for data. Controlling these permissions protects both your privacy and the privacy of the people you know.

How to Protect Yourself:

1. Open your device's privacy settings.
2. Review which apps have access to your contacts.
3. Turn off contact access for apps that do not require it.
4. Review which apps can access your photos or media.
5. Select **Only Selected Photos** or **No Access** whenever possible.
6. Avoid auto-sync features that upload your photos to unknown cloud services.
7. Turn off "Find friends using contacts" in social media apps if available.

Examples:

1. A messaging app may request your entire contact list. You can add people manually instead.
2. A social media app may ask for full photo access just to post one picture. Choose **Select Photos Only**.
3. A dating app might upload your contacts to suggest matches. Turning off access prevents this.

If It Happens:

1. Revoke contact and photo permissions for the app.
2. Check the app's account settings and delete any contact lists it uploaded.
3. Review your cloud storage to confirm no photos were auto-uploaded.
4. Remove location data (metadata) from photos before sharing, if possible.
5. Let close contacts know if their information may have been exposed.

Key Idea:

Your contacts and photos are personal. Only allow access when it is clearly necessary.

70. Limit Who Can Tag You in Photos

What It Means:

When others tag you in photos, those images may become visible to people you do not know. Tags can reveal where you were, who you were with, and details about your routines. Even innocent photos can expose personal information. Limiting who can tag you protects your privacy and keeps your social presence under your control.

How to Protect Yourself:

1. Go to your social media privacy settings
2. Turn on the option that requires **your approval** before a tag appears on your profile
3. Change tagging settings to **Only Me**, **Friends Only**, or **No One,** depending on your comfort level
4. Avoid being tagged in photos that show your home, workplace, daily routine, or children
5. Ask friends and family not to tag you automatically, especially in public posts

Examples:

1. A group photo from a party gets posted, and someone tags you. With approvals turned on, you can choose whether it shows on your profile
2. Someone tags you in a photo showing your neighborhood or street. You can decline the tag to avoid exposing your location
3. A co-worker posts a work event picture and tags you. Approvals allow you to control what appears professionally

If It Happens:

1. Remove any tags from photos you do not want connected to your name
2. Report or request the removal of photos that violate your privacy
3. Adjust your tagging settings so you must approve all future tags
4. Review your profile and remove old, tagged photos that no longer represent you
5. If someone repeatedly tags you without consent, consider muting, unfollowing, or blocking them

Key Idea:

Tagging should be your choice. You decide what shows up under your name online.

71. Turn Off Contact Syncing in Apps

What It Means:

Some apps ask to "sync your contacts" so they can help you find friends or connect with people you know. What really happens is that these apps upload your entire contact list to their servers. This means your family, coworkers, doctors, and personal connections may be stored, analyzed, or shared for advertising. Turning off contact syncing keeps your relationships private.

How to Protect Yourself:

1. Open your device's **Settings**, then go to **Privacy**
2. Select **Contacts** and review which apps have access
3. Turn off access for apps that do not need your contact list
4. Open each social app and disable "Sync Contacts" or "Upload Contacts" in the app settings
5. Avoid using "Find Friends Automatically" features
6. Whenever an app asks to access your contacts, choose **No**

Examples:

1. A social media app asks to sync contacts so it can suggest friends. You can skip that step and still use the app
2. A messaging app wants your contacts to auto-fill phone numbers. You can add contacts manually instead
3. A shopping or gaming app requests contact access. There is no reason to need that information, so deny it

If It Happens:

1. Turn off contact syncing in the app immediately
2. Go into the app's account settings and **delete uploaded contacts** if the option is available
3. Change passwords for your account if you see suspicious suggestions or friend requests
4. Inform close contacts if you think their information may have been shared
5. Check for future app updates because some apps re-enable syncing by default

Key Idea:

Your contact list is personal and private. Do not allow apps to upload or store it unless it is truly necessary.

72. Be Careful With QR Codes

What It Means:

QR codes are quick and convenient, but they can also be used to trick you. A QR code can send you to a fake website, download a harmful app, or start a payment without you noticing. Because you cannot see where a QR code leads until you scan it, scammers use them to hide dangerous links.

Being cautious with QR codes keeps your devices and accounts safe.

How to Protect Yourself:

1. Only scan QR codes from trusted sources like businesses you recognize or official signage
2. Avoid scanning QR codes found on random flyers, stickers, or public places
3. Before opening the link, **check the URL** displayed on your screen
4. If the link looks strange or unfamiliar, **do not open it**
5. Avoid making payments or entering passwords through QR codes unless you are sure of the source
6. Use your phone's built-in QR scanner instead of third-party scanner apps you do not trust

Examples:

1. A scammer places a fake QR code over a parking meter QR. You scan it, and it leads to a phishing payment page
2. A restaurant menu QR code is safe because it is part of an official business environment
3. A QR code inside a text message claims you need to scan it to "verify your account." Do not scan it

If It Happens:

1. If you open a suspicious link, close the page immediately
2. Do not enter any personal information, passwords, or payment details
3. Clear your browser history and cookies
4. Run a security scan on your phone
5. Change passwords for any accounts that may have been affected
6. Monitor your bank and payment apps for unusual transactions

Key Idea:

Look before you scan. QR codes are helpful only when you trust their source.

73. Do Not Share Boarding Pass Photos

What It Means:

A boarding pass may look harmless, but it contains more information than most people realize. The barcode on your boarding pass can reveal your full name, flight details, frequent flyer number, and sometimes even your passport information. Scammers can use this to access your travel accounts, change your flight, or gather personal data about you.

Sharing boarding pass photos online puts your identity and travel plans at risk.

How to Protect Yourself:

1. Never post photos of your boarding pass on social media
2. Keep your boarding pass in a secure place while traveling
3. Dispose of used boarding passes by shredding them, not just throwing them away
4. Avoid leaving digital copies of boarding passes stored in shared email or photo albums
5. If traveling with others, make sure they also understand the risk

Examples:

1. Someone posts a boarding pass on Instagram. A scammer scans the barcode and logs into their airline account
2. A lost or discarded boarding pass is found in an airport. A criminal uses the passenger record to change seats or flights
3. A traveler shares a boarding pass photo while still at the airport, revealing the exact time and location of their travel

If It Happens:

1. Log in to your airline or travel account immediately and change your password
2. Turn on two-factor authentication for your travel accounts
3. Contact the airline and ask them to review your booking for unauthorized changes
4. Check your frequent flyer rewards balance and protect your points
5. Monitor your email and travel apps for suspicious activity

Key Idea:

Your boarding pass is not just a travel document. It is a key to your personal travel identity. Keep it private.

74. Disable Ad Tracking and Personalized Advertising

What It Means:

Posting your daily habits may seem harmless, but it can reveal patterns about your life. What time you leave home, when you return, where you go, where you work out, or where your kids go to school. Someone with bad intentions can use this information to predict when you are away, where to find you, or how to target you.

Your routine is personal. Keeping it private keeps you safe.

How to Protect Yourself:

1. Avoid posting the same activities at the same time every day
2. Turn off location tagging on photos and videos
3. Share photos after you leave a place, not while you are still there
4. Do not openly mention your work schedule, commute, or school drop-off times
5. Be careful with check-ins on apps that show where you are
6. Switch personal social media accounts to private whenever possible

Examples:

1. Posting a daily gym routine at 6 AM every morning shows when your home is empty
2. Sharing a photo every day when you arrive at work shows your location and schedule
3. Recording your walk route every evening shows your predictable movement pattern

If It Happens:

1. Delete or hide posts that reveal your routine
2. Change your posting habits so they are less predictable
3. Adjust privacy settings to limit who can see your activity
4. Review your follower list and remove people you do not know or trust
5. If someone is trying to follow or track you, block and report them immediately

Key Idea:

Your routine is valuable information. Keep it private to protect your safety and peace of mind.

75. Be Aware of Location Data Hidden in Photos

What It Means:

When you take a photo with your phone, it often stores information called **metadata**. This can include the exact GPS location where the photo was taken. If you upload or share that photo publicly, someone could use that data to learn where you live, where your children go to school, where you shop, or other personal locations. You may not see the location info, but it can be extracted easily.

Protecting your photo metadata helps keep your private life private.

How to Protect Yourself:

1. Turn off **Location Services** for your camera app in your phone settings
2. Before sharing photos, use your device's **Remove Location Data** option if available
3. Use messaging apps or social media settings that automatically remove location metadata
4. Avoid posting photos that show identifiable personal surroundings, like house numbers or street signs
5. Review old photos on your profile and remove any that may reveal sensitive locations
6. If you use cloud storage, check whether location data is being stored or shared

Examples:

1. A photo taken in your living room may contain GPS data showing your exact home address
2. A first-day-of-school picture could reveal the school's location
3. A vacation photo posted while you are still away can show that your home is empty at that moment

If It Happens:

1. Remove or delete any photos that expose your location
2. Turn off camera location settings going forward
3. Review your social media accounts and hide older albums
4. Ask friends or family to remove photos of you that reveal private locations
5. If you believe your address was exposed publicly, monitor for suspicious messages, mail, or unwanted visitors

Key Idea:

Photos can reveal more than just memories. Remove location data to keep your private spaces protected.

CHAPTER 6
Protect Your Social Life and Reputation

76. Think Before Responding to Toxic Messages

What It Means:

Online conversations can get emotional quickly. When someone sends a rude, aggressive, or disrespectful message, reacting immediately can make the situation worse. Pausing gives you space to respond calmly or choose not to engage at all. Protecting your peace is more important than winning an argument.

How to Protect Yourself:

1. When you receive a negative message, wait before replying
2. Ask yourself if responding is necessary or helpful
3. If the message is clearly toxic, choose not to reply at all
4. Mute, block, or restrict the person if their behavior continues
5. Save your energy for respectful conversations
6. If the message is threatening, report it to the platform

Examples:

1. Someone sends a rude comment on social media. You pause, decide it isn't worth your time, and ignore it
2. A coworker sends a sharp message while upset. You wait and respond later, calmly and professionally
3. A stranger tries to start an argument online. You block and move on without engaging

If It Happens:

1. Do not replay the argument in your mind. Let it go
2. If the message affected your mood, step away from your phone or computer for a moment
3. Talk to someone supportive if the situation bothers you

4. Block or mute the person if they continue to send negativity
5. If harassment becomes constant or threatening, report it or seek assistance

Key Idea:

You do not have to respond to everything. Protect your peace by choosing when and whether to engage.

77. Avoid Arguing With Strangers Online

What It Means:

Online arguments rarely end with understanding or agreement. Most strangers on the internet are not looking to listen or learn. Many want to provoke reactions. Engaging in arguments can waste time, raise stress, and damage your reputation. Walking away is not losing. It is choosing peace and protecting your mental energy.

How to Protect Yourself:

1. If someone tries to start an argument online, pause before responding
2. Ask yourself whether your reply will truly change anything
3. If the conversation shifts into disrespect, stop responding immediately
4. Use the **mute**, **restrict**, or **block** features on social platforms
5. Avoid debating sensitive topics with people you do not know personally
6. Remember that not every opinion requires your response

Examples:

1. A stranger comments on your post to provoke you. You ignore it and move on
2. Someone attacks your point of view in a public thread. You decide the conversation is not worth your time and exit
3. A person online keeps pushing your buttons. You block them and protect your peace

If It Happens:

1. Leave the conversation immediately
2. Take a short break from your device if you feel frustrated

3. Block or mute the person to prevent future interactions
4. Avoid reading back through the argument. Delete or hide the thread if needed
5. Remind yourself that your time and energy are valuable

Key Idea:

Your attention is valuable. Do not waste it on arguments that do not improve your life.

78. Do Not Overshare During Emotional Moments

What It Means:

Strong emotions can make us say more than we intend. When you are upset, stressed, or frustrated, it can feel natural to vent online. But once something is posted, it becomes hard to take back. Oversharing in emotional moments can reveal personal details, damage relationships, or be used against you later. Giving yourself time to calm down protects your reputation and peace of mind.

How to Protect Yourself:

1. If you feel emotional, avoid posting or messaging immediately
2. Write your thoughts in a private journal or notes app instead of online
3. Talk to a trusted friend or family member instead of posting publicly
4. Set a personal rule: do not post when angry, sad, or overwhelmed
5. Review posts before sending and ask, "Will I still feel good about this tomorrow?"
6. Remember that privacy cannot be restored once something is shared online

Examples:

1. You had a bad day at work. Instead of posting about coworkers, you call a friend and vent privately
2. You are going through a breakup. Instead of writing emotional posts online, you take time to process your feelings
3. You get into an argument in messages. You pause and come back later with a calmer response

If It Happens:

1. Delete or hide the emotional post as soon as possible
2. Apologize privately if someone was affected or hurt
3. Review your privacy settings to reduce who can see your future posts
4. Reflect on what triggered the emotional response and how to handle it differently next time
5. Consider stepping away from social media until your emotions settle

Key Idea:

Feelings pass. But posts stay. Protect your privacy by pausing before you share.

79. Keep Personal Conversations Private

What It Means:

Some conversations are meant to stay between you and the other person. When private discussions are shared publicly, screenshotted, or forwarded, misunderstandings grow and trust is broken. Protecting your private conversations helps maintain healthy relationships and prevents personal information from spreading where it does not belong.

How to Protect Yourself:

1. Have sensitive conversations in private messages, not public comment sections
2. Avoid discussing personal issues inside group chats where messages can be misinterpreted
3. Before sending a voice message or video, ask if it is a good time for the other person
4. Do not forward private messages to others without permission
5. Store screenshots in a secure, private location if you need them for legal or safety reasons
6. If a conversation becomes emotional, consider moving to a phone call instead of texting

Examples:

1. A friend shares something personal with you privately. You keep it between the two of you out of respect
2. You are upset at someone. Instead of venting in a group chat, you speak to them directly in a calm moment
3. Someone tries to pressure you into sharing screenshots. You refuse because you value trust and dignity

If It Happens:

1. If someone shared your private conversation, tell them clearly that it was not acceptable
2. Limit what you share with that person going forward
3. Remove your personal messages or data from group chats if possible
4. If the issue escalates into harassment or bullying, block and report the person
5. If needed for your safety, keep copies of messages privately as documentation

Key Idea:

Privacy builds trust. Protect your conversations the same way you protect your personal information.

80. Know How to Block and Report Accounts

What It Means:

Not everyone online has good intentions. Some people may try to bother you, pressure you, insult you, or make you feel uncomfortable. Blocking and reporting are tools that help you protect yourself. Blocking stops someone from contacting you. Reporting lets the platform know about harmful behavior so they can take action.

Knowing how to use these tools keeps your online space safe and respectful.

How to Protect Yourself:

1. Learn where the **Block** and **Report** buttons are for the apps you use most
2. Block anyone who makes you uncomfortable, not just people who are rude
3. Report accounts that are abusive, impersonating others, or sending threats
4. Do not explain yourself to someone you blocked. You do not owe them a conversation
5. Use **mute** or **restrict** if you want to limit interactions without entirely blocking
6. Teach children and family members how to block and report too.

Examples:

1. A stranger repeatedly messages you, even after you ignore them. You block them immediately
2. Someone impersonates your friend's account and asks for money. You report it for fraud
3. A person leaves rude or disrespectful comments on your posts. You delete the comments and block them

4. You see hate speech in a community group. You report the post and leave the discussion

If It Happens:

1. Block the person right away to stop any future contact
2. Take screenshots before blocking if you need evidence for safety or reporting
3. Report the account to the platform, choosing the correct category (harassment, spam, impersonation, etc.)
4. Review your privacy settings and tighten who can view or message you
5. If threats are serious or personal, contact local authorities for support

Key Idea:

Blocking is not rude. It is healthy. You deserve to feel safe and respected in every space, including online.

81. Set Boundaries With Online Communities

What It Means:

Online groups, forums, fan pages, and social circles can be fun and supportive. But if you spend too much time on them or share too much personal information, you may feel pressure to fit in, respond constantly, or reveal more than you intended. Boundaries help you stay in control of your time, privacy, and emotional well-being.

You decide how close or distant you want to be in online spaces.

How to Protect Yourself:

1. Choose communities that feel respectful and positive
2. Do not share personal details such as your address, job location, finances, or relationships
3. Limit how much time you spend in group chats or forums per day
4. Mute conversations or leave groups that drain your energy
5. Avoid posting when you are tired, stressed, or emotional
6. Remember: you do not owe anyone explanations about your personal life

Examples:

1. You enjoy a hobby group, but the chat becomes overwhelming. You mute notifications and check in once a day
2. A community asks for personal details to "get to know you." You share only general interests instead of sensitive information
3. A group conversation becomes negative. You quietly leave and prioritize your peace

If It Happens:

1. Step back and take a break from the community
2. Review what personal information you may have shared and remove posts if possible
3. Adjust your privacy settings or change usernames if needed
4. If someone from the group continues to contact you privately, block or restrict them
5. Reflect on what boundaries you want to maintain moving forward

Key Idea:

You control your participation. Online communities should support your life, not overwhelm it.

82. Be Careful When Sharing Opinions Publicly

What It Means:

Sharing your thoughts online can feel natural, but public posts can spread far beyond your intended audience. Opinions shared in the moment can be misunderstood, taken out of context, or shown to people you never expected. Once something is public, it can be saved, shared, or reposted without your control. Being thoughtful about what you share protects your reputation and relationships.

How to Protect Yourself:

1. Pause before posting and ask yourself if this opinion needs to be public
2. Consider whether the post could be misunderstood by people who do not know you well
3. Avoid posting when you are emotional, frustrated, or tired
4. If your opinion relates to personal beliefs, keep the audience limited to people you trust
5. Use private group chats for deeper conversations instead of public comment sections
6. Remember that once posted, even deleted messages can be screenshotted and shared

Examples:

1. You have a strong opinion about a news story. Instead of posting publicly, you discuss it with close friends in private
2. You disagree with someone's post. You choose not to respond publicly because it could turn into an argument
3. You avoid commenting on sensitive topics in work-related spaces to protect your professional reputation

If It Happens:

1. If you regret a post, delete it quickly
2. If the post causes conflict, address the misunderstanding privately and calmly
3. Review your privacy settings and adjust who can see your posts
4. Apologize directly if someone was harmed, rather than making a public apology
5. If old posts resurface, acknowledge the growth and clarify your current stance

Key Idea:

Your voice is valuable, so use it with intention. Think before sharing publicly to protect your peace and your reputation.

83. Do Not Post When You Are Angry

What It Means:

Anger can make us speak faster than we think. When we post online while upset, we may say things we do not truly mean or share more information than we should. Once something is posted, it can be copied, screenshotted, and shared, even if you delete it later. Choosing not to post while angry protects your relationships, reputation, and peace.

How to Protect Yourself:

1. If you feel angry, put your phone down before responding
2. Give yourself time to cool off, even just a few minutes
3. Write your thoughts in a private note, not in a message or comment box
4. Do not respond to messages or notifications while your emotions are intense
5. Return to the situation later with a calm mind
6. If needed, speak to the person privately instead of publicly

Examples:

1. Someone leaves a rude comment on your post. Instead of responding instantly, you step away and decide to ignore or block them
2. You receive a message that hurts your feelings. You write a draft reply, but wait an hour before sending, and soften the tone
3. You feel misunderstood in a group chat. You leave your phone for a bit and return it when you feel clearer

If It Happens:

1. Delete emotional posts as soon as possible
2. Apologize privately if you say something hurtful

3. If screenshots were taken, acknowledge the mistake and show maturity, not defensiveness
4. Reflect on what triggered your anger before it escalated
5. Make a personal rule to step away from your device when emotions are high

Key Idea:

Anger is temporary. A post can be permanent. Protect your future by waiting before you react.

84. Avoid Posting Work Conflicts or Issues

What It Means:

Work frustrations are typical, but posting about them online can create serious consequences. Even if you do not mention your company by name, small details can reveal where you work. Employers, coworkers, and clients can see your posts, and misunderstandings can grow. Keeping work-related conflicts offline protects your job, your professional reputation, and your future opportunities.

How to Protect Yourself:

1. If you are upset about work, talk privately with someone you trust instead of posting online
2. Keep your personal social media accounts separate from your professional identity
3. Avoid sharing details about coworkers, office problems, customers, or internal decisions
4. Think before posting: "Would I be comfortable if my boss or HR read this?"
5. Handle workplace issues directly through the proper channels instead of public spaces
6. If you need support, use a private journal, therapist, or close friend rather than an online audience

Examples:

1. You had a stressful day at work. Instead of posting publicly, you take a walk or message a close friend
2. A coworker upsets you. You address the situation privately and respectfully when emotions are calm
3. A company decision frustrates you. You avoid tweeting about it and speak with your manager if needed

If It Happens:

1. Delete the post immediately, even if you think no one saw it
2. If someone was directly affected, offer a private and sincere apology
3. Reflect on what led you to post and what you can do differently next time
4. Increase privacy settings on your social accounts to limit who can view your posts
5. If the situation escalates, speak with HR or a supervisor calmly and professionally

Key Idea:

Your professional reputation is valuable. Protect it by keeping work matters off social media.

85. Protect Your Professional Reputation Online

What It Means:

Your online presence can influence job opportunities, business relationships, and how others view your character. Employers, clients, and colleagues often search your name online before working with you. What they find should reflect professionalism, maturity, and respect. Protecting your professional reputation means being mindful of what you post and how you interact.

How to Protect Yourself:

1. Search your name online to see what others can find about you
2. Delete or hide old posts that no longer reflect who you are
3. Keep your personal and professional accounts separate when possible
4. Use a clean profile photo and bio on platforms you use for work
5. Avoid engaging in online arguments, gossip, or drama
6. Share content that reflects your skills, interests, and positive values
7. If you have a LinkedIn profile, keep it updated and consistent with your professional goals

Examples:

1. Before applying for a job, you review your social media and remove old posts that seem unprofessional
2. You avoid commenting on controversial discussions using your real name or work profile
3. You use LinkedIn to share achievements, learning experiences, and professional insights

If It Happens:

1. Delete or hide posts that could hurt your reputation
2. If misinformation is spreading, correct it calmly and privately where possible
3. If something damages your reputation, address it respectfully and take accountability if needed
4. Strengthen your online presence with positive, thoughtful posts over time
5. Ask trusted friends or mentors for feedback on how your online presence appears

Key Idea:

Your professional reputation is built through consistent actions. Protect it by staying thoughtful and intentional with your online presence.

86. Verify People Before Meeting Them in Person

What It Means:

The internet makes it easy to meet new people, but not everyone is who they claim to be. Before meeting someone in person from social media, dating apps, online marketplaces, or group chats, it is crucial to confirm their identity. This protects your safety and prevents dangerous situations.

How to Protect Yourself:

1. Ask for their full name and verify it through a quick online search
2. Confirm that their social media profiles look genuine (not recently created or empty)
3. Video call before meeting to confirm they are who they say they are
4. Meet in a public place where other people are around
5. Tell a trusted friend where you are going and who you are meeting
6. Arrange your own transportation so you can leave at any time
7. If anything feels strange, cancel the meeting. Your safety comes first.

Examples:

1. Someone from a marketplace app wants to pick up an item at your home. You meet in a public place instead
2. A dating app match refuses a video call. That is a sign to stop communication
3. A new online friend seems friendly, but their profile has no real photos or posts. You choose not to meet

If It Happens:

1. If you meet someone and feel unsafe, leave immediately and go to a public area
2. Block them on all platforms if anything about the interaction felt wrong
3. Report their account to the app or website you connected through
4. If personal information was shared, increase your privacy settings and monitor your accounts
5. If you were threatened or harmed, contact authorities and seek help right away

Key Idea:

Trust is built, not assumed. Always verify people before meeting them in real life.

87. Do Not Share Screenshots of Private Chats

What It Means:

Private conversations are based on trust. Sharing screenshots without permission can embarrass someone, damage relationships, or cause misunderstandings. Even if the conversation seems harmless, once a screenshot is shared, you lose control of who sees it. Keeping private chats private protects your integrity and the trust of others placed in you.

How to Protect Yourself:

1. Treat private messages as confidential unless you have a real safety reason to share them
2. If someone says something meaningful or essential, ask for permission before sharing
3. Avoid sending screenshots to group chats because messages can spread quickly
4. Remember that sharing messages during conflict can escalate the situation
5. Use judgment. If you are unsure whether to share something, do not share it
6. If a conversation involves sensitive personal topics, keep it between the two of you

Examples:

1. A friend tells you something personal. You keep it private rather than posting or forwarding it.
2. Someone trusts you with something emotional. You show respect by not repeating it
3. A misunderstanding happens in a group. Sharing chats would make it worse, so you address the issue privately.

If It Happens:

1. If you shared something you regret, delete it and apologize directly.
2. Acknowledge the mistake without excuses.
3. Rebuild trust through consistent, respectful behavior.
4. If someone shared your messages without permission, set clear boundaries and limit future sharing.
5. Remove that person from sensitive conversations going forward.

Key Idea:

Trust is built through privacy and respect. If it was said in private, keep it private.

88. Be Cautious in Online Dating

What It Means:

Online dating can help you meet new people, but it also comes with risks. Some people misrepresent themselves, while others may attempt scams, emotional manipulation, or physical harm. Being cautious helps you enjoy the experience while protecting your safety, privacy, and well-being.

How to Protect Yourself:

1. Use reputable dating apps that verify identity or profiles
2. Do not share personal details too quickly, such as your address or workplace
3. Video chat before meeting in person to confirm they match their profile
4. Arrange to meet in a public place for the first several dates
5. Tell a trusted friend who you are meeting, where, and when
6. Pay for your own transportation so you can leave at any time
7. If someone tries to rush intimacy, commitment, or trust, slow down and reassess

Examples:

1. Someone insists on meeting at your home for the first date. You decline and suggest a public café instead
2. A match asks for money or says they are in an emergency. You recognize this as a scam and block them
3. Someone avoids video calling and makes excuses. You choose to end communication

If It Happens:

1. If a dating interaction makes you uncomfortable, block and stop contact immediately
2. Report fake profiles or harassment through the app
3. If you share personal information, increase your privacy settings, and be cautious with future communication
4. If you feel unsafe or threatened, reach out to local authorities or a trusted support person
5. Take time to reflect and return to dating only when you feel grounded and confident

Key Idea:

Your safety comes first. Online dating should add to your life, not put you at risk.

89. Keep Personal and Work Profiles Separate

What It Means:

Your personal and professional lives do not need to mix online. Keeping separate profiles helps protect your privacy, maintain professionalism, and reduce the chance of misunderstandings at work. Your personal opinions, humor, or lifestyle may not be appropriate for colleagues or clients to see. Separation creates healthy boundaries.

How to Protect Yourself:

1. Use one account for personal friends and family, and a different one for work or professional networking
2. Keep your professional profile clean, respectful, and focused on your skills and work experience
3. Avoid adding bosses, coworkers, or clients to personal social media unless you truly trust them
4. Adjust privacy settings so only selected people can view your personal posts
5. Use different profile photos for personal and professional accounts to avoid confusion
6. Be mindful of what you post on any platform where your real name is used

Examples:

1. You use LinkedIn for your career and keep Facebook or Instagram for personal connections
2. You avoid posting about personal stress or conflicts on an account your coworkers can see
3. You keep hobbies, humor, and private discussions away from work-related platforms

If It Happens:

1. Review your followers and remove or restrict anyone who should not see personal content
2. Adjust privacy settings on personal accounts to limit who can view posts
3. Delete or hide posts that colleagues may misinterpret
4. If a misunderstanding occurs, address it calmly and clearly
5. Going forward, maintain a clear line between personal and professional spaces

Key Idea:

Separating personal and professional profiles protects your privacy, reputation, and peace of mind.

90. Teach Children How to Be Safe Online

What It Means:

Children use the internet for school, games, videos, and socializing. They may not understand the risks of sharing personal information or talking to strangers. Teaching them early builds lifelong habits that protect them from scams, bullying, and harmful situations.

How to Protect Them:

1. Talk openly about internet safety in a calm and supportive way
2. Explain that personal information like full name, address, phone number, and school should never be shared online
3. Teach them to check with an adult before downloading apps or clicking links
4. Encourage them to tell you immediately if something online makes them uncomfortable
5. Set screen time boundaries so online activity does not replace real-world friendships
6. Use parental controls when needed, but combine them with communication, not secrecy
7. Teach them that not everyone online is who they say they are

Examples:

1. You help your child set up a game account using a nickname instead of their real name
2. A stranger tries to chat with them in a game.
3. Your child sees a message that feels rude or scary. They know they can come to you without getting in trouble.

If It Happens:

1. If your child shares personal information, have them change usernames or adjust privacy settings.
2. If they experienced online bullying, block the person and report the account to the platform.
3. If they clicked a suspicious link, scan the device for malware and change any passwords
4. If they communicate with someone pretending to be someone else, stop contact and talk through what happened in a supportive way.
5. Reinforce that they are not in trouble. They need to feel safe coming to you.

Key Idea:

The most powerful safety tool is trust. Teach your child that you are someone they can turn to. Safety starts with communication, patience, and guidance.

CHAPTER 7
Protect Your Home and Family

91. Do Not Share Photos Showing Your Home Layout

What It Means:

Photos taken inside your home can reveal more than you realize. The background may show your floor plan, security devices, expensive items, or entry points. Someone with malicious intent could use these details to learn how to break in or locate valuable possessions. Protecting your privacy means being mindful of what your photos show.

How to Protect Yourself:

1. Before posting a photo or video, look carefully at the background
2. Avoid showing doorways, hallways, or the general layout of your home
3. Do not display expensive items like electronics, jewelry, or artwork
4. Take photos against simple backgrounds like plain walls when possible
5. If you want to share family moments, consider taking them outdoors or in non-identifiable spaces
6. Blur or crop anything that reveals too much detail

Examples:

1. You take a mirror selfie. You crop out the doorway behind you, so your home layout is not visible
2. You want to share your living room decoration. You take the photo close-up instead of wide-angle
3. A video call shows too much background. You use a virtual background or reposition your camera

If It Happens:

1. If you posted a photo that reveals your home layout, delete it immediately
2. Check comments to ensure no personal details were saved or shared by others
3. If the photo was shared widely, update door locks and home security just to be safe
4. Avoid posting new photos of your home layout going forward
5. Talk with family members so everyone understands not to post revealing images

Key Idea:

Your home is a private space. What you show online should not give strangers a map to it.

92. Do Not Post School Locations or Bus Stops

What It Means:

Sharing where your child goes to school or where they wait for the bus can put them at risk. Strangers could learn about their daily routine, and someone with bad intentions could use that information to approach them. Keeping school and travel routes private protects your child's safety.

How to Protect Yourself:

1. Do not post photos of school buildings, school signs, or bus stops online
2. Avoid tagging the school's name in posts or sharing location check-ins
3. If your child wears a school uniform, avoid showing logos or school names in photos
4. If you want to celebrate school achievements, share general statements without specific identifying details
5. Have family members follow the same privacy rules
6. Talk to children about never sharing school or travel details online

Examples:

1. Your child receives an award. You post a photo of the award itself, not inside the school
2. You want to share a "first day of school" photo. You take the picture at home, not in front of the school sign
3. A friend tags your child's school. You kindly ask them to remove the tag or post

If It Happens:

1. Delete any posts showing school names, signs, uniforms, or bus stops
2. Change privacy settings so only trusted people can see future family posts
3. Inform your child's school about any safety concerns if the information is widely shared
4. Teach your child not to tell strangers where they go to school
5. Monitor who follows your accounts and remove anyone you do not recognize

Key Idea:

Your child's safety is more important than social media moments. Protect their routine, and you protect them.

93. Use Parental Controls for Children's Devices

What It Means:

Children are naturally curious, and the internet contains both helpful and harmful content. Parental controls let you control what children can see, who they can talk to, and how long they can use their devices. These tools are not about spying or punishment. They are about protection and teaching healthy digital habits.

How to Protect Your Family:

1. Set up parental controls on phones, tablets, computers, and smart TVs
2. Use age-appropriate content filters to block harmful or explicit material
3. Limit screen time to ensure children balance online and offline activities
4. Restrict in-app purchases to prevent accidental spending
5. Monitor which apps are installed and remove apps that are unsafe
6. Review chat and messaging features to make sure they are appropriate
7. Place devices in shared spaces rather than bedrooms whenever possible

Examples:

1. You use built-in smartphone controls to limit time on social apps
2. Your child wants to download a new game. You check that it is safe before approving
3. You restrict YouTube to the kids' version, so only child-friendly videos appear

If It Happens:

1. If your child accesses inappropriate content, stay calm and talk through what happened
2. Adjust parental controls to be more potent and more specific
3. Have an open conversation about why certain content is unsafe
4. Remove unsafe apps and block websites as needed
5. Reinforce that they are not in trouble. You are guiding them, not punishing them.

Key Idea:

Parental controls work best when combined with honest conversations. Safety is built through guidance, trust, and consistent support.

94. Teach Family to Recognize Scams

What It Means:

Scams are everywhere online. Scammers use phone calls, emails, text messages, and social media to trick people into giving away money, personal information, or account access. Teaching your family how scams work helps protect everyone in your home.

How to Protect Your Family:

1. Explain that scammers often pretend to be banks, delivery companies, government agencies, or familiar brands
2. Teach everyone to be suspicious of messages that create urgency or pressure
3. Show them how to spot spelling mistakes, strange email addresses, or unusual links
4. Make it a rule: never send money, gift cards, or personal information to strangers online
5. If a message feels suspicious, encourage family members to ask someone they trust before acting
6. Practice saying no to pushy requests or emotional pressure

Examples:

1. A family member receives a text saying their bank account is locked. Instead of clicking the link, they check their bank app or call the official customer service number
2. Someone online claims they need money urgently. Your family member recognizes this as a manipulation tactic and does not send anything

3. A child gets a pop-up saying they won a prize. They now know that real prizes do not ask you to pay a fee to claim them

If It Happens:

1. If personal information was shared, change passwords immediately
2. If money was sent, contact the bank or payment service to try to stop the transaction
3. Report the scam to the platform where it occurred (email provider, social media, etc.)
4. Block the scammer's account or phone number
5. Talk about the situation calmly so no one feels ashamed. Use it as a learning moment

Key Idea:

Awareness is protection. The more your family understands scams, the safer everyone becomes.

95. Secure Your Home Wi-Fi Network

What It Means:

Your home Wi-Fi is the gateway to all your connected devices. If someone gains access to it, they could monitor your activity, steal your personal information, or even control your smart devices. Securing your network makes it much harder for intruders to access your digital life.

How to Protect Your Home Wi-Fi:

1. Change the default Wi-Fi name (SSID) to something neutral that does not reveal personal information
2. Create a strong, unique Wi-Fi password that is difficult to guess
3. Use **WPA2** or **WPA3** security (never use open or WEP)
4. Log in to your router settings and change the default admin username and password
5. Turn off **Guest Network** access unless you need it
6. If you use a guest network, give it a different password from your main network.
7. Make sure your router firmware is updated regularly.
8. Place your router in a central location to reduce signal leaking outside your home when possible

Examples:

1. You rename your Wi-Fi from "SmithFamilyHome" to something non-identifiable like "GreenSky"
2. You create a strong password that combines letters, numbers, and symbols instead of using your phone number or address
3. When guests visit, you give them access through a separate guest network rather than your main one

If It Happens:

1. If you think someone has access to your Wi-Fi, change the Wi-Fi password immediately
2. Change the router admin password and check connected devices in the router settings
3. Remove unfamiliar devices from the network
4. Update your router's firmware and security settings
5. Consider upgrading to a newer router with stronger security if your current one is outdated

Key Idea:

Your Wi-Fi is the doorway to your home. Keep the lock strong.

96. Rename Your Wi-Fi to Something Neutral

What It Means:

Your Wi-Fi name (also called the SSID) can reveal information about you without you realizing it. Names like "BrownFamilyHome" or "Apartment 3B" can expose your identity or location. Changing your Wi-Fi name to something neutral keeps your household private and reduces targeted attacks.

How to Protect Yourself:

1. Avoid using your last name, address, apartment number, school, workplace, or hobbies
2. Choose a simple, non-personal Wi-Fi name such as GreenForest, BlueSignal, CloudZone, and RiverConnect.
3. Log in to your router's settings to update the network name
4. If you change the Wi-Fi name, your devices will need to reconnect, so plan a few minutes to update them
5. Keep the name professional and non-distracting to avoid drawing attention

Examples:

1. Instead of "JohnsonFamilyWiFi," you rename it to "SilverSky."
2. Instead of "Apt12B_WiFi," you use "MorningWave"
3. You avoid funny or rude names that could attract unwanted attention or neighbors trying to connect.

If It Happens:

1. If your Wi-Fi name currently reveals something personal, change it right away
2. If neighbors or strangers have been connecting to your Wi-Fi, also change your password

3. Check your router settings to remove any unknown devices
4. Reset your network security mode to **WPA2** or **WPA3** for extra protection
5. Continue to avoid personal information in future Wi-Fi names

Key Idea:

A neutral Wi-Fi name keeps your identity and daily life private from anyone nearby or scanning for networks.

97. Keep Security Camera Feeds Private

What It Means:

Home security cameras can protect your home, but if they are not set up securely, others could access the live feed. This could let strangers watch inside your home, see when you are away, or learn your daily routines. Keeping camera feeds private protects your home and your family.

How to Protect Yourself:

1. Change the default username and password for your camera system
2. Use a strong, unique password that is not used for any other account
3. Turn on two-factor authentication if the camera app offers it
4. Make sure your home Wi-Fi network is secured with WPA2 or WPA3
5. Disable any feature that makes your camera feed public or searchable
6. Keep your camera software and mobile app updated
7. Only share camera access with trusted family members

Examples:

1. You buy a new doorbell camera and change the default login information before using it
2. You restrict who can view your camera feed so only your household has access
3. You avoid connecting your security camera to public Wi-Fi or guest networks

If It Happens:

1. Change the camera login password immediately
2. Change your Wi-Fi password and remove any unknown devices from the network
3. Turn on two-factor authentication if it was not enabled before
4. Check if the camera has been moved, rotated, or changed settings without your permission
5. If you believe someone was watching your feed, contact the camera manufacturer for further assistance

Key Idea:

Security cameras protect your home, but only if access to them is tightly controlled. Your home's privacy is worth guarding.

98. Avoid Sharing Illness, Travel, or Family Emergencies Publicly

What It Means:

When you share personal situations such as being sick, traveling, or dealing with family emergencies online, you may unintentionally signal that your home is empty or that you are vulnerable. Strangers or criminals could use this information to target you or your family. Keeping these details private protects your safety and peace during stressful times.

How to Protect Yourself:

1. Avoid posting about travel plans before or during the trip.
2. Share vacation photos after you return home.
3. If you are dealing with an illness or medical situation, share updates only with people you trust
4. Do not announce when you are home alone
5. Keep family emergency details private to avoid emotional exploitation
6. If someone asks for information, share only what feels safe and necessary

Examples:

1. Instead of posting "Leaving for vacation today," you wait until you return and post your best photos.
2. You do not share hospital updates online, but you keep family and close friends updated privately.
3. Instead of saying "I'm home alone for the weekend," you go about your regular routine offline.

If It Happens:

1. If you posted travel or illness details, delete or edit the post
2. Ask friends not to tag your location or mention your situation publicly
3. If you feel your home may now be vulnerable, increase security (lights, locks, neighbor awareness)
4. Review your privacy settings and limit who can see future posts
5. Reflect on what details you want to keep private moving forward

Key Idea:

Your personal life is not public content. Protect your safety by sharing life updates thoughtfully and at the right time.

99. Have a Family Safety Word for Emergencies

What It Means:

A family safety word is a simple code word that everyone in your household knows but is never shared publicly. It is used to confirm identity in situations where someone may try to trick or pressure a family member. This word helps children and adults quickly recognize whether a message, request, or pickup is truly safe.

How to Protect Your Family:

1. Choose a word that is easy to remember but hard for others to guess
2. Make sure all family members understand when the word should be used
3. Practice using the word in simple examples to build confidence
4. Remind children that they should never share the word with friends, teachers, or online contacts
5. Update the word if someone outside the family learns or guesses it
6. Keep the word consistent across phone calls, text messages, and in-person situations

Examples:

1. A child is waiting to be picked up from school. If someone other than a parent arrives, the child asks for the family safety word
2. A teenager receives a text saying, "I need you to send money. I lost my phone." They ask for the safety word and verify it before responding
3. A family member receives a call claiming to be a relative in trouble. You ask for the safety word to confirm whether the situation is real

If It Happens:

1. If a stranger knows the safety word or guesses it, change it immediately
2. Explain to children that the new word must stay private
3. Talk calmly about what happened and reinforce how the safety word protects everyone
4. Review real-life situations where the safety word might be needed
5. Continue practicing it once in a while so everyone remembers

Key Idea:

A family safety word provides quick, silent protection. It helps every member of your household stay safe, even when you are apart.

100. Store Important Documents Securely

What It Means:

Important documents contain personal information that can be used to steal your identity, open accounts in your name, or access your finances. Keeping these documents safe protects your identity and your future.

How to Protect Yourself:

1. Keep physical documents like passports, birth certificates, Social Security cards, and financial records in a secure place such as a locked drawer or safe
2. Use a **fireproof and waterproof safe** for your most critical items
3. Scan documents and keep digital copies stored in secure, password-protected cloud storage or on an encrypted drive
4. Do not carry sensitive documents in your purse, backpack, or wallet unless necessary.
5. Shred any documents that have your name, address, or personal numbers before throwing them away
6. Review your stored documents once a year and remove anything outdated or no longer needed

Examples:

1. You store your birth certificate and passport in a locked safe at home instead of leaving them in a desk drawer
2. You scan your medical records and keep them encrypted, instead of emailing them around
3. You shred old tax forms instead of throwing them in the regular trash

If It Happens:

1. If a document is lost or stolen, report it immediately (passport, driver's license, security numbers, etc.)
2. Freeze your credit to prevent identity theft
3. Monitor your bank and credit statements for unusual activity
4. Notify your financial institutions if your personal information may be at risk
5. Replace lost documents through official government channels

Key Idea:

Your documents tell your life story. Protect them like they protect you.

101. Review Your Online Safety Habits Regularly

What It Means:

Cybersecurity is not something you set once and forget. Technology changes. Scams evolve. Apps update. Reviewing your online safety habits regularly helps you stay protected as the digital world shifts. Small check-ins throughout the year can prevent big problems later.

How to Protect Yourself:

1. Schedule a reminder every 3 to 6 months to review your privacy and security settings
2. Update your passwords and remove accounts you no longer use
3. Check which apps have access to your camera, microphone, contacts, and location
4. Review social media posts and delete anything that shares too much personal information
5. Make sure your devices, browsers, and antivirus software are all up to date
6. Reflect on any situations where you felt uncomfortable online and adjust your habits accordingly

Examples:

1. Every January and July, you spend 30 minutes reviewing your passwords and removing old accounts
2. You check app permissions after installing new apps to make sure they are not accessing unnecessary data
3. You look at your social media profiles the way a stranger would and remove anything overly personal

If It Happens:

1. If you discover a security risk (like an old account or weak password), fix it right away
2. If a device is out of date, install updates or replace it if necessary
3. If you notice suspicious activity on any account, change the password and enable two-factor authentication
4. If you realize you have been oversharing, delete posts and tighten your privacy settings
5. Let this become a habit that grows stronger over time

Key Idea:

Online safety is a lifestyle, not a one-time task. Checking in regularly keeps you protected, confident, and in control.

CONCLUSION

If you've made it to this point, take a moment to appreciate that. Most people move through the online world hoping nothing bad happens to them. You decided to learn how to protect yourself, and that choice matters.

We live in a time where being online is part of everyday life. We bank online, stay in touch with friends online, work online, shop online, and store our memories online. Because of that, your digital security is not something separate from your real life. It *is* part of your real life. Your identity, your privacy, your money, your reputation, and your peace of mind all exist in the digital space, too.

A lot of people think cybersecurity is only for professionals, or that you have to be "tech-savvy" to stay safe. That is not true. Most of the time, people get scammed or hacked not because they are careless, but because no one ever taught them what to watch out for. This book was written to change that.

The steps you learned are not complicated. They are not technical. They are everyday habits. You don't have to master everything at once. Just start with one habit, then add another, and another. Over time, these small actions build absolute protection.

Maybe today, you will update one password.

Maybe tomorrow, you turn on two-factor authentication.

Maybe next week, you can talk to your family about online scams.

That is progress. That is a strength.

And if something has already happened to you, that does not mean you failed. Scammers and cybercriminals are skilled at what they do. What matters is what you choose to do next. Fix what you can, learn what you didn't know before, and move forward with more awareness.

The most essential idea to bring with you is this:

You deserve to feel safe and confident online.

Your personal information matters.

Your privacy matters.

Your peace of mind matters.

Keep reviewing the habits in this book. Come back to them. Make them routine. And when you're ready, share what you learned with someone else. When you protect yourself, you also help protect the people around you.

This is not about fear.

It is about control, understanding, and confidence.

You are now much more prepared than most people online. And you did that by taking one step at a time.

Let this be the start of a safer digital life you can trust.

UNDERSTANDING AI IN CYBERSECURITY

To understand how AI affects online safety, we should first examine each idea separately.

Artificial Intelligence (AI) is when computers are designed to learn and make decisions in ways that resemble human thinking. AI doesn't just follow instructions written by a programmer. It learns from data and patterns. The more information it sees, the better it gets. For example, AI can:

1. Suggest videos, games, or music you might enjoy based on your past choices
2. Predict what you are trying to type when you text
3. Recognize your face to unlock your phone or tag people in photos

AI improves over time because it keeps noticing what people do and how they behave. This helps it make better guesses and decisions.

Cybersecurity is the practice of protecting personal information, accounts, devices, and online identities from being accessed or misused by others. Cybersecurity includes many skills and habits, such as:

1. Creating strong passwords
2. Avoiding online scams
3. Keeping software updated
4. Recognizing suspicious messages and links

In simple terms: AI helps computers learn. Cybersecurity helps keep you safe. When these two areas come together, the results can be both helpful and risky.

How AI Helps With Safety

AI supports cybersecurity in many ways. It is especially good at noticing patterns and detecting changes that humans may overlook. AI can:

1. Detect hacking attempts faster than a person
2. Warn you if your account is logged into from an unusual location
3. Block dangerous websites, files, or links before you click them
4. Notice unusual spending patterns and alert your bank

AI can analyze vast amounts of information in seconds. This makes it very useful for protecting systems and people.

How AI Can Be Used to Trick People

However, the same technology that protects us can also be used to deceive us. Attackers can use AI to:

1. Write fake messages that sound natural and personal
2. Copy someone's writing style by studying their posts online
3. Create realistic voice recordings of someone you know
4. Produce fake photos or videos that look real

In the past, many scams were easy to identify because they sounded strange or had obvious spelling mistakes. Today, AI can make scams look professional and familiar. A message might sound like it came from a friend, teacher, or family member. A voice message might sound real, even if it is entirely fake. The danger is not how obvious the scam appears, but how believable it feels.

Why Awareness Matters

Most of us use the internet daily. We message friends, watch videos, do homework online, and share parts of our lives on social media. As a result, we leave digital footprints, such as photos, comments, and posts. AI can study these footprints. It can learn how you talk, what you care about, and who you interact with. That is why someone using AI to scam you may seem like they know you.

Being aware means understanding that not everything online is what it appears to be. Trust is important, but so is caution.

How to Recognize AI-Based Scams

Instead of only looking for spelling mistakes or awkward wording, pay attention to the situation. Ask yourself:

1. Is someone trying to make me act fast or make an emotional decision?
2. Is someone asking for money, passwords, or codes?
3. Is someone contacting me in a way they normally wouldn't, such as by text instead of in person?
4. Is the message trying to stop me from checking with someone else first?

AI-driven scams often try to create urgency or fear. They want you to react quickly, so you don't think. If something feels rushed or uncomfortable, pause before responding.

How to Protect Yourself

You don't need special training. Protection mostly comes from consistent, simple habits:

1. Use strong passwords and avoid using the same password for multiple accounts.
2. Turn on two-factor authentication for important accounts.
3. Never share verification codes with anyone, even if the message sounds real.

4. If something feels suspicious, contact the person another way to confirm.
5. Be thoughtful about what personal details you share online, including birthdays, school details, and travel plans.

These habits help create natural barriers that protect your information and identity.

If You Think You Were Tricked

If something goes wrong, do not panic. Respond quickly and take control:

1. Change your passwords right away.
2. Turn on two-factor authentication if it is not already on.
3. Check your recent account activity for unfamiliar devices or logins.
4. If money was involved, contact your bank immediately.
5. Report the situation to the platform or website so they can secure your account.

Acting fast can prevent further damage and protect your information.

QUICK-START SAFETY GUIDE

If You Only Have 15 Minutes, Start Here

These are the five quickest steps that give you strong protection with the least effort. No tech skills required. No paid software. Just steady action.

These steps immediately strengthen your identity, secure your accounts, protect your privacy, and reduce the chances of being hacked or impersonated.

Think of this as locking your front door before we reinforce the rest of the house.

Step 1: Turn On Two-Factor Authentication

Time Required: About 2 minutes

Two-factor authentication (2FA) adds an extra step to your login. Even if someone gets your password, they still can't access your account without the extra code.

Why It Matters: Most account breaches occur because passwords are leaked or reused. 2FA blocks those attacks.

How To Do It:

1. Open your account's Security or Login settings.
2. Turn on Two-Factor Authentication.
3. Choose an Authenticator App (Google Authenticator, Microsoft Authenticator, etc.).
4. Save the backup codes somewhere safe.
5. **Do This First For:**
6. Your primary and backup email accounts
7. Your banking and financial apps
8. Your social media accounts

Step 2: Change Your Most Important Password

Time Required: About 3 minutes

You don't need to fix every password now. Just change the one that matters most: your email password.

Why Email Matters: If someone gains access to your email, they can reset your passwords, impersonate you, and access your private information.

Create a Strong Password That Is:

1. Long (14+ characters)
2. Unique (not used anywhere else)
3. Easy to remember, hard to guess
4. **Use a simple phrase:**

- mycatlikes2sleepallday!
- SummerCoffeeNightDrive2024

Step 3: Turn Off Ad Tracking and Location History

Time Required: About 3 minutes

Your phone tracks where you go, what you search, and what you buy. Turning this off protects your privacy immediately.

How To Do It:

1. iPhone: Settings → Privacy → Tracking → Turn off "Allow Apps to Request to Track"
2. Android: Settings → Privacy → Ads → Turn off "Ad Personalization"
3. Turn off Ad Personalization in Google/Apple account settings
4. Turn off Personalized Ads inside social media apps

Step 4: Remove One Old Account You Don't Use

Time Required: 3–5 minutes

Old accounts are one of the most significant hidden risks because old passwords often end up in data leaks.

How To Do It:

1. Search your email for "Welcome," "Verify your account," or "Reset password."
2. Find one account you no longer use.
3. Log in and delete it.
4. If deletion isn't possible, change the password to something unique.

Step 5: Turn On Automatic Updates

Time Required: 1 minute

Updates fix security weaknesses before attackers can use them.

How To Do It:

- On your phone: Settings → Software Update → Turn on Automatic Updates
- On your computer: Turn on automatic updates for the system and apps

You Just Increased Your Safety Immediately

You now have stronger identity protection, safer accounts, reduced tracking, and a solid foundation to build on.

Take a breath.

You are already safer than most people online.

REAL-LIFE STORIES THAT SHOW WHY ONLINE SAFETY MATTERS

1. The social media quiz that revealed too much

Lisa liked light and fun posts. She answered personality quizzes on social media because they were quick and often gave her a laugh. Over time, she filled out dozens of them, and many of the questions were about childhood details. She thought those answers were private, even when she posted them publicly. Months later, she received an alert that someone tried to reset her primary email password. The reset method asked for answers to routine security questions. The attacker used details that matched answers Lisa had shared in public quizzes.

Fortunately, Lisa still had access and was able to lock down her accounts. She changed her passwords, removed public answers, and updated her security questions to use passphrases, not real facts. The panic she felt that night stayed with her for weeks.

Lesson

1. Sharing seemingly harmless personal trivia can expose you to account takeover.
2. Treat quiz answers as public information and never use real answers for security questions.
3. Use long, unique passwords and two-factor authentication where available.

Key insight

Small, playful posts add up into a profile that can be used against you.

2. The old password that came back years later

Marcus had been using the same short password since high school. Back then, he only used it for a gaming site. As years passed, he reused that password across several services because it was convenient. He did not realize that a breach at the game site had released thousands of credentials. Months later, attackers tried the leaked combinations on popular services, and several of Marcus's accounts were compromised. They posted spam from his social pages and made small purchases using stored payment methods.

Marcus felt ashamed that he had not taken password hygiene seriously. He spent a long weekend changing passwords, enabling two-factor authentication, and moving all credentials into a password manager. He also cleaned up spam posts and contacted the companies involved to have the charges reversed.

Lesson

1. Reused passwords create a chain of vulnerability.
2. One leaked password can unlock many accounts.
3. Use a password manager and unique passwords for each site.

Key insight

Security is only as strong as your weakest password.

3. The phone left on the cafe table

Daniel was in a hurry and left his phone on the café table when he placed his order. He returned within a minute and assumed everything was fine. Later that day, he noticed unusual bank alerts and messages he did not send. Somebody had briefly picked up his unlocked phone, opened apps that were signed in, and copied sensitive information. Daniel had used his Notes app for quick lists and sometimes stored passwords there.

After the incident, he felt exposed and angry. He took immediate steps. He remotely locked and wiped the device, changed key passwords, and moved sensitive data to a password manager. He began treating his phone like a wallet. He set the phone to lock more quickly and avoided leaving it unattended for even a short time.

Lesson

1. Even short unattended moments can lead to significant consequences.
2. Use automatic screen lock and do not store passwords in plain text on a phone.
3. Install device tracking and remote wipe features.

Key insight

Physical access, however brief, is a significant risk when devices are unlocked.

4. The fake bank call that sounded real

Julia received a call that seemed urgent. The person on the line used her name and the last four digits of her account. The caller said they noticed suspicious activity and asked her to verify a one-time code that arrived by text. Julia read the code aloud. The caller used it immediately to reset passwords and to move funds. By the time she realized the call was fraudulent, significant money had been withdrawn. Julia was devastated and embarrassed. She called her bank and reported the fraud. The bank froze the accounts and began a recovery process.

In the days that followed, she learned how social engineering works and why it is dangerous to confirm codes or reveal security details to callers. She now calls the bank back on an official number whenever a call seems suspicious.

Lesson

1. Legitimate institutions do not ask you to read codes to strangers on the phone.
2. If a caller pressures you to act now, pause and verify independently.
3. Keep official numbers handy and contact your bank directly through their published number.

Key insight

Urgency and partial knowledge are the tools of social engineering.

5. The photo that revealed the address

A couple posted a proud photo of their new TV with family gathered around. The post was public because they wanted friends to see it. Later, a neighbor messaged to say they recognized a street sign reflected in a window behind the group. The recognition led to a break-in at the couple's house while they were out. The couple had not intended to share their location, but details in the shot combined into an identifying clue. They learned to check backgrounds before posting and to crop or blur anything that could reveal addresses, house numbers, or unique exterior features. They also tightened home security after the incident.

Lesson

1. Photo backgrounds can leak location or private details you may miss.
2. Review and crop photos carefully before you post.

3. Delay sharing travel or “I am away” posts until you are safely home.

Key insight

Images often tell a story you did not mean to publish.

6. The work rant that would not go away

After a stressful week, Maria posted a candid message about frustrations at work. It felt cathartic at the moment. A coworker took a screenshot and shared it with management. Weeks later, the post was mentioned in a performance conversation and used to question her professionalism. Maria did not intend harm, but she underestimated how quickly messages can spread online. She learned to write a journal privately when she needed to vent and to take time before posting anything that might reflect on her career. Over time, she rebuilt relationships at work and used direct conversations rather than public posting to resolve problems.

Lesson

1. Expressing frustration on social media can have professional consequences.
2. Step away and write privately if you feel emotional; revisit later before sharing.
3. Use private channels for workplace concerns.

Key insight

The internet amplifies raw emotion and stores it longer than you expect.

7. The free airport Wi Fi trap

Jason connected to the free, open Wi-Fi at the airport to check a quick email and pay a bill. The network required no password and looked legitimate. Unknown to him, another user on the same network was intercepting traffic. The interceptor captured session data and used it to access accounts. Jason noticed unauthorized transactions later that day. He contacted his bank, had the fraudulent charges reversed, and changed his passwords. After that trip, he chose to use his phone hotspot or a trusted VPN whenever he was on public networks. He now treats open networks as untrusted by default.

Lesson

1. Attackers can monitor open networks.
2. Use a VPN or mobile hotspot for sensitive actions.
3. Avoid banking or account changes on public Wi Fi.

Key insight

The convenience of public Wi Fi comes with a real security cost.

8. The romance scam that felt real

Nadia matched with someone online who invested time in conversation and built trust slowly. He shared stories, remembered small details, and checked in often. After weeks of messaging, he described an urgent family crisis and asked for money. Because trust had been established, Nadia made a transfer. The person then stopped responding, and the identity unraveled. She felt foolish, but the experience showed how emotional manipulation works. She reported the person, blocked them, and spoke to a friend and to her bank about protecting herself. She learned to pause before sending money to anyone online and to verify details independently.

Lesson

1. Scammers build trust over time to lower your guard.
2. Never send money to someone you have not met and verified.
3. Ask neutral questions and verify their story through independent channels.

Key insight

Trust is earned, but online relationships can be built to exploit it.

9. The fake job offer

Evan received what appeared to be a polished job offer. The recruiter asked him to purchase equipment up front and promised reimbursement. The scheme was professional-looking and even used a copy of a company website. After he paid, the reimbursements never arrived, and the contacts vanished. Evan reported the incident and warned others in online job groups. From then on, he carefully reviewed job offers, used official company contact information, and refused to pay for positions. He also learned to look for red flags such as requests for money, poorly written contracts, or emails from free webmail addresses.

Lesson

1. Real employers do not require applicants to pay for equipment to start work.
2. Verify offers through official company channels and look for independent confirmation.
3. Research recruiters and check for reviews or warnings online.

Key insight

If a job requires you to pay to start, it is likely a scam.

10. The child who shared too much

A parent posted a cute photo of their child wearing a school uniform with the school logo visible. A stranger was able to identify the school and neighborhood. The parent had not meant harm, but it opened a worry about privacy and safety. They moved to private sharing with close family and friends, removed identifying details from captions, and talked to their child about why certain information should not be posted publicly. The family also set friend lists to limited audiences and used privacy settings to control who sees posts.

Lesson

1. Others can use children's photos and identifying details to track location.
2. Share children's images privately and remove identifiers from public posts.
3. Teach kids appropriate privacy habits as they grow.

Key insight

Protecting children online is a deliberate step that families can plan for.

11. The notes app password list

Tasha stored all her passwords and recovery answers in a plain Notes file because it was quick. When her phone was stolen, the thief used the content to access several accounts. Even though she used two-factor authentication, enough accounts were vulnerable that the thief accessed her email and social accounts. Tasha spent days recovering accounts and felt violated that private details were so exposed. She moved all credentials to a reputable password manager, set a strong master passphrase, and enabled biometric locks. She learned that convenience without encryption is risky.

Lesson

1. Do not store passwords in plain-text apps on phones.
2. Use encrypted password managers and protect the master key.
3. Enable device security and remote wipe.

Key insight

Convenience is no substitute for encryption and proper security tools.

12. The contact sync surprise

James installed a new messaging app that asked for permission to sync contacts. He gave access without thinking. The app used his address book to suggest his number to a wide range of other users. Colleagues and acquaintances he had not spoken to in years received invitations. He felt uncomfortable with how broadly his number spread. He removed contact sync, changed app permissions, and reached out to trusted people to explain. From then on, he reviewed permissions more carefully and kept contact syncing off unless necessary.

Lesson

1. Grant permissions deliberately, not by habit.
2. Contact syncing can spread your details to unknown parties.
3. Review app permissions after installation.

Key insight

Permissions matter because apps can share your network without your explicit consent.

13. The boarding pass photo

Sam posted a proud photo of his boarding pass to show he was traveling for a dream trip. Someone zoomed in on the image, scanned the QR code or booking reference, and used it to access parts of his airline booking. They changed seat assignments and modified preferences. While the attacker did not cause severe harm, the incident revealed how barcodes and boarding passes contain private data. Sam now avoids posting images of tickets, boarding passes, or screenshots that show codes or booking numbers. He also checks account security settings with travel providers and enables two-factor authentication where offered.

Lesson

1. Boarding passes and QR codes encode sensitive information.
2. Do not share images of travel documents publicly.
3. Use provider account security features to protect bookings.

Key insight

Digital codes are private. Once published, they can be used by anyone.

14. The smart camera left unsecured

A family installed smart cameras to feel safer. They kept the default admin password for the router and the camera accounts. Later, they discovered someone could access the live feeds online. The feeling of safety disappeared. The experience taught them to change default passwords, use strong, unique router credentials, segment the network with a guest Wi Fi for IoT devices, and keep firmware updated. They also reviewed camera settings and limited cloud sharing. After tightening access, they regained security and peace of mind.

Lesson

1. Change default passwords on smart devices immediately.
2. Keep firmware updated and isolate IoT devices on a guest network.
3. Review cloud sharing settings and access logs.

Key insight

Smart home devices are convenient, but only secure if you configure them correctly.

15. The emotional post that stayed forever

Anthony posted a long, emotional message after a breakup. It felt like a release at the time. Later, he regretted the tone and detail. Even after deleting the post, friends and strangers had saved screenshots. The message resurfaced months later in a way that embarrassed him. He now uses a private journal and offline support when he is vulnerable. He learned to delay public sharing until emotions are settled and to consider the long-term effects of posts he might later regret.

Lesson

1. Emotional posts can have permanent consequences.
2. Pause before posting and consider private outlets for raw feelings.
3. Assume anything you post could be saved by others.

Key insight

Feelings can hit hard and make everything seem immediate, but the internet doesn't move on as fast as we do. A post made in a moment of emotion can outlast that moment by months or even years. That gap between how we feel now and how long things stay online is where regret often shows up.

EMERGENCY PLAYBOOK

Emergency Playbook 1: Account Hacked

Goal: Regain control fast.

Do this now

1. Try to sign in.
2. If you can sign in, change the password immediately to a unique one.
3. Turn on two-factor authentication.
4. Sign out of all devices from the account's security page.
5. Remove unfamiliar devices and connected apps.

If you cannot sign in

1. Use "Forgot password."
2. Choose recovery by email or an authenticator app. Avoid SMS if possible.
3. If recovery fails, submit an account recovery form on the provider's help page.

After you regain access

1. Check recent logins and locations.
2. Verify recovery email and phone number.
3. Regenerate backup codes.
4. Review and remove unknown third-party app access.

Emergency Playbook 2: Phone Lost or Stolen

Goal: Protect data and locate the device.

Do this now

1. Use Find My iPhone or Find My Device to locate.
2. Mark lost to lock the screen and show a contact number.

3. Erase the device remotely if you see risky movement or cannot recover it.
4. Change passwords for email and banking that were used on the device.
5. Remove the device from the trusted devices lists on major accounts.

If you suspect theft

1. Contact your carrier to suspend the SIM.
2. File a police report with the device serial or IMEI.
3. Contact your employer if it is a work device.

Emergency Playbook 3: Clicked a Phishing Link or Entered Your Password

Goal: Contain the damage and secure accounts.

Do this now

1. Disconnect from public Wi-Fi. Use a cellular or a trusted network.
2. Close the page. Do not interact further.
3. Change the password for the affected account from a known good device.
4. Turn on two-factor authentication for that account.
5. If you reused that password anywhere, change those passwords.

If you downloaded a file or installed an extension

1. Remove the file or browser extension.
2. Run a full malware scan with a reputable tool.
3. Restart the device after the scan.

Report

1. Report the phishing message inside the email or platform.
2. If it was a work email or device, notify your IT team.

Emergency Playbook 4: Ransomware or "Your Files Are Encrypted"

Goal: Stop the spread and begin recovery.

Do this now

1. Disconnect the device from the internet and any external drives.
2. Do not pay the ransom.
3. Take a photo of the ransom note for reference.
4. Use a clean device to change passwords for email and cloud storage.
5. Contact your IT team if this is a work device.

Recovery

1. Restore files from a known good backup made before the incident.
2. If no backup, consult a reputable incident response or local professional.
3. Wipe and reinstall the operating system from official media.
4. Reinstall apps from official stores only.
5. Apply all updates before reconnecting to networks.

Emergency Playbook 5: Sudden Loss of Cell Service or SIM Swap Suspected

Goal: Regain number control and protect accounts.

Do this now

1. Try calling your own number from another phone.
2. If calls go to someone else or you have no service, contact your carrier immediately.
3. Ask the carrier to lock your account and require an in-person photo ID or account PIN for changes.
4. From a different device, change passwords for email, bank, and major accounts.
5. Switch two-factor authentication to an authenticator app or security key.

After service is restored

1. Review account recovery settings and remove your phone number where possible.
2. Generate new backup codes for key accounts.

Emergency Playbook 6: Identity Theft Signs Appear

Goal: Stop new fraud and document the case.

Do this now

1. Place a fraud alert with a credit bureau.
2. Freeze your credit at all major bureaus.
3. Download your credit reports and review for unknown accounts or inquiries.
4. Contact companies where fraud occurred and close or flag accounts.

Documentation

1. File an identity theft report with the appropriate authority in your country.
2. Keep copies of reports, letters, emails, and case numbers in one folder.

Follow up

1. Set calendar reminders to recheck reports in 30 days and 90 days.

Emergency Playbook 7: Private Photos or Data Posted Without Consent

Goal: Remove content and preserve evidence.

Do this now

1. Take screenshots with timestamps and URLs for evidence.
2. Use the platform's reporting tool for non-consensual content.
3. Submit takedown requests to all locations where it appears.
4. Block the uploader and avoid responding.

If there are threats or extortion

1. Contact local authorities and provide evidence.
2. Tell a trusted person for support and safety planning.

After removal

1. Set up alerts for your name and usernames to catch reposts.

Emergency Playbook 8: Unauthorized Bank or Card Charge

Goal: Limit loss and replace credentials.

Do this now

1. Lock the card in your bank app if available.
2. Call the number on the back of the card. Dispute the charge and request a new card number.

3. Review recent transactions and flag all suspicious ones.
4. Change your bank app and email passwords.

If you stored the card online

1. Remove the card from shopping sites and apps.
2. Turn on transaction alerts for every charge.
3. Consider a temporary credit freeze if there are multiple events.

Emergency Playbook 9: Someone Is Impersonating You Online

Goal: Take down fake accounts and warn contacts.

Do this now

1. Capture screenshots of the profile and URL.
2. Report the account as impersonation using the platform's form.
3. Ask friends to report the account as well.
4. Post a short notice from your real account that a fake profile exists.

If the impersonation is used for fraud

1. Inform your bank and credit card issuers if money requests were sent.
2. File a report with the appropriate authority if required by your region.

Emergency Playbook 10: Home Wi-Fi May Be Compromised

Goal: Regain control of the network and protect devices.

Do this now

1. Unplug the router for 30 seconds, then power it back on.
2. Log in to the router admin page from a wired or trusted device.
3. Change the router admin password to a strong, unique one.
4. Update the Wi-Fi network password and use WPA2 or WPA3.
5. Disable WPS if it is enabled.

Clean up

1. Remove unfamiliar devices from the client list.
2. Update router firmware.
3. Create a separate guest network for visitors and smart home devices.
4. Change key account passwords used on that network.

RESOURCES

You don't need to use every tool on this list, and you definitely don't need to use everything at once. Think of these as helpful options you can come back to whenever you're ready. The goal is not to overwhelm you. The goal is to give you reliable choices when you need them.

Password Security and Account Protection

1. 1Password / Bitwarden (Password Managers)

A password manager helps you create and store strong passwords, so you don't have to remember them. These tools automatically fill in your passwords when needed, and they keep everything encrypted.

If you've been using the same few passwords for years, this is where you start.

2. Have I Been Pwned, https://haveibeenpwned.com

This website lets you check whether your email or password has been part of a data breach. If it has, change the password immediately on every site where you use it.

3. Authy or Google Authenticator (Two-Factor Authentication)

These apps generate a code you enter when signing into accounts. Even if someone steals your password, they still can't get in without the code.

4. YubiKey or Titan Security Key (Physical Security Keys)

This is a small device you plug into your computer or phone when logging in. It's the strongest form of account protection available today.

Use a key like this for your email, bank, and social media accounts.

Email and Private Communication

5. ProtonMail / Tutanota

These are email services that do not sell, track, or scan your inbox. If privacy matters to you, these are worth switching to, especially for banking, legal, and medical accounts.

6. Signal

A private messaging app that encrypts conversations so no one else can read them, not companies, not hackers, and not your phone provider.

It works just like texting, so no technical knowledge is needed.

7. SimplePractice: Avoid SMS Verification for Important Logins

Text messages can be intercepted. When possible, use authentication apps or security keys instead of SMS codes.

Safer Web Browsing

8. Firefox or Brave Browser

These browsers prioritize privacy more than Chrome. They block many trackers automatically.

9. DuckDuckGo or Startpage (Private Search Engines)

These search engines don't record your search history or build a profile about you.

10. uBlock Origin (Tracker and Ad Blocker)

This browser extension blocks hidden tracking scripts that follow you around the internet. It also automatically blocks many scam-looking ads.

11. Privacy Badger

Works alongside uBlock Origin to stop companies from tracking you across websites.

12. HTTPS Everywhere

Ensures you always connect to websites securely when available.

Device and Computer Protection

13. Windows Defender / Bitdefender / Malwarebytes

These are reliable antivirus tools. If you use Windows, Windows Defender is built in and completely free, and it works well when kept up to date.

14. FileVault (Mac) / BitLocker (Windows)

These encrypt your computer so that if it's lost or stolen, your files remain locked and unreadable.

15. Ninite.com (Safe Software Installation)

This website lets you download commonly-used apps without hidden toolbars, trackers, or unwanted extras.

If you've ever installed an app and ended up with five new toolbars, this prevents that.

16. Onyx (Mac) or CCleaner (Windows)

Helpful if your device feels slow or cluttered. Use these tools carefully and sparingly to clean system junk.

Identity and Financial Protection

17. AnnualCreditReport.com

You can legally request your credit reports for free every year. Check them for accounts you don't recognize.

18. Credit Freeze (Equifax, Experian, TransUnion)

Freezing your credit is one of the strongest ways to stop identity theft. It prevents anyone from opening accounts in your name.

19. Identity Monitoring (Only If Needed)

If you've been a victim of identity theft, consider reputable monitoring services — not the ones pushed by spammy ads.

Stick with your bank, Apple, Google, or Microsoft before third-party companies.

20. Bank Transaction Alerts

Turn on alerts for every purchase. If someone uses your card, you'll know right away.

Home, Family, and Real-Life Digital Safety

21. Google Family Link / Apple Screen Time

Helps you guide children's online behavior without spying or punishing. You can set limits, block inappropriate apps, and teach healthy digital habits.

22. Router Settings

Change your home Wi-Fi password and network name from the default.

A default network name can reveal your router type, potentially exposing security weaknesses.

23. Smart Home Privacy Settings

If you have smart speakers, security cameras, or connected devices, review their privacy settings. Turn off microphones and cameras when not needed.

24. Stop Oversharing Emergencies or Travel Plans Online

Thieves and scammers monitor social media posts for opportunities. Share vacation photos *after* your return.

Learning and Awareness

25. Cybersecurity and Fraud Education Resources

- FTC Consumer Alerts (United States)
- FBI Internet Crime Complaint Center (IC3)
- Your bank's fraud education page
- YouTube channels focused on scam awareness

26. Practice Digital Awareness Conversations with Family

Talk about scams the same way families talk about fire safety, calmly and openly. Awareness is one of the strongest forms of protection.

ABOUT THE AUTHOR

Ousmane Barry, PhD, is a U.S. Army Veteran and cybersecurity professional with more than ten years of hands-on experience in digital security, data protection, and cyber risk management. He holds a PhD in Cybersecurity Management with a specialization in Artificial Intelligence and Machine Learning, two Master's degrees in Computer Science and Cybersecurity, and a Bachelor's degree in Computer Science. His background enables him to explain complex cybersecurity concepts in a practical, relatable, and easy-to-apply way.

Dr. Barry holds well-respected industry certifications, including CompTIA Security+, Certified Ethical Hacker (CEH), Certified Information Security Manager (CISM), Project Management Professional (PMP), CompTIA SecurityX, and AWS Certified Solutions Architect Associate (SAA-C03). He has supported organizations in banking, healthcare, education, and government, helping them build stronger defenses against digital threats.

Before beginning his cybersecurity career, Dr. Barry served in the United States Army. His time in service shaped his discipline, leadership approach, and commitment to protecting others. These values remain at the core of his work today.

Outside of security consulting, Dr. Barry is also an author. He writes to empower individuals and families by making cybersecurity easier to understand and apply. His teaching style focuses on real-life examples, clear guidance, and confidence-building steps. His goal is not only to help people protect themselves but to help them feel in control of their digital world.

His mission is simple: to help people stay safe, informed, and confident online.

Stay Connected with Dr. Barry

1. LinkedIn: @drbarryofficial
2. Instagram: @drbarryofficial
3. X: @drbarryofficial
4. TikTok: @drbarryofficial

www.ingramcontent.com/pod-product-compliance
Lightning Source LLC
LaVergne TN
LVHW101615210926
848480LV00010B/1449
* 9 7 9 8 2 1 8 8 6 8 6 0 4 *